Noël Coward & Radclyffe Hall

Between Men ~ Between Women

Lesbian and Gay Studies

Lillian Faderman and Larry Gross, Editors

Noël Coward & Radclyffe Hall

KINDRED SPIRITS

TERRY CASTLE

COLUMBIA UNIVERSITY PRESS
New York

Columbia University Press
New York   Chichester, West Sussex
Copyright © 1996 Columbia University Press
All rights reserved
Library of Congress Cataloging-in-Publication Data
Castle, Terry.
Noel Coward and Radclyffe Hall : kindred spirits / Terry Castle.
p.   cm.
Includes bibliographical references (p.   ) and index.
ISBN 0-231-10596-7 (cloth). — ISBN 0-231-10597-5 (pbk.)
1. Coward, Noel, 1899–1973—Friends and associates.
2. Homosexuality and literature—Great Britain—History—20th
century.   3. Gays' writings, English—History and criticism.
4. Authors, English—20th century—Biography.   5. Hall, Radclyffe—
Friends and associates.   6. Coward, Noel, 1899–1973—Influence.
7. Actors—Great Britain—Biography.   8. Gays—Great Britain—
Biography.   9. Hall, Radclyffe—Influence.   10. Lesbians in
literature.   11. Gay men in literature.   I. Title.
PR6005.O85Z623   1996
820.9'00912–dc20   96–22750
CIP

Casebound editions of Columbia University Press
books are printed on permanent and durable acid-free paper.
Printed in the United States of America
c 10 9 8 7 6 5 4 3 2 1

To stephen, with love

Contents

Acknowledgments

I would like to thank the librarians at the Harry Ransom Humanities Research Library at the University of Texas, their counterparts at the Stanford University Libraries, the Theatre Museum in Covent Garden, Michael Imison Playwrights Ltd., and Miss Enid Foster of the Garrick Club for graciously allowing me to examine various books and manuscripts during the writing of this book.

I am likewise extremely grateful to everyone—in particular the archivists at the Hulton-Deutsch Picture Library and Richard Mangan at the Mander and Mitchenson Theatre Collection—who loaned photographs for reproduction. Finally, I would like to thank several friends and colleagues who helped along the way: Tamara Bernstein, Joe Bristow, Bridget Castle, Jennifer Crewe, Susan Gubar, renée hoogland, Polly Kummel, Margo Leahy, Linda Long, M. Mark, Nancy K. Miller, Randy Nakayama, Susan Pensak, Marjorie Perloff, Rob Polhemus, Lou Roberts, Beverley Talbott, Mary Ann Tilotta, John Tinker, and especially Stephen Orgel.

Noël Coward &
Radclyffe Hall

Noël Coward & Radclyffe Hall

KINDRED SPIRITS

It is hard at first glance to think of two homosexual personalities of the 1920s with less in common than Noël Coward and Radclyffe Hall. Close if not exact contemporaries (she was born in 1880 and he in 1899, but both came to public notice in the years immediately following the First World War), the two seem to mark out between them the abyss separating male and female homosexual sensibilities in Britain in the pre-Wolfenden era. Coward, whose string of brilliant stage hits, *London Calling!* (1923), *The Vortex* (1924), *Hay Fever* (1924), *Fallen Angels* (1925), *This Year of Grace* (1928), and *Private Lives* (1930), made him the most sought-after actor-playwright of his generation, was forced, out of harsh necessity, to keep his homosexuality a secret for almost all his working life. His carefully evolved stage persona—the clipped, epigrammatic delivery, the silver cigarette holders and perfectly tailored dinner jackets, the air of slightly louche world-weariness—was also, one suspects, an ironic defense: a useful protective shield in a society that still imprisoned male homosexuals and subjected them to public vilification. Through innuendo or the well-judged, fleetingly campy aside, one might satirize hypo-critical social codes obliquely without risking self-incrimination. And at this subliminal provocation Coward was eminently success-ful: his remarkable career as actor, singer, composer, novelist, play-wright, cabaret performer, and general arbiter of fashionable taste for more than fifty years might indeed be said to represent the single most sustained homosexual infiltration of mainstream Anglo-American culture of the century.[1]

Radclyffe Hall, by contrast, though openly lesbian from her early years, faced no such direct threat to livelihood or personal safety, even after the publication of her notorious apologia for female homosexuality, *The Well of Loneliness*, in 1928. *The Well* itself might be banned—and in fact was proscribed in England until 1949 under the Obscene Publications Act of 1885—but the novelist her-self was not in danger of arrest or incarceration: unlike male homo-sexuality, lesbianism was never a crime in Great Britain.[2] Invisible in the eyes of the law, Hall had no need to resort to the irony and indi-rection that became Coward's witty stock-in-trade. Indeed, the very invisibility of female homosexuality in official English culture seems to have animated her fierce desire to propagandize on the subject in *The Well of Loneliness*. Her style is for the most part the antithesis of Coward's—painfully discursive, polemical, almost entirely devoid of gaiety, archness, or ambiguity. Where he is fey, she seems driven; when she agonizes, he simply lifts an eyebrow. It's like comparing a glass of champagne to an aspersion of bitters.

One could easily draw out the contrast at Hall's expense. Consider, for example, this fairly typical passage from *The Well*, on the suffering of those cursed (like the heroine Stephen Gordon) with the "terrible nerves of the invert":

> Pacing restlessly up and down her bedroom, Stephen would be
> thinking of Angela Crossby—haunted, tormented by Angela's

words that day in the garden: 'Could you marry me, Stephen?' and then by those other pitiless words: 'Can I help it if you're—what you obviously are?'

She would think with a kind of despair: 'What am I in God's name—some kind of abomination?' And this thought would fill her with very great anguish, because, loving much, her love seemed to be sacred. She could not endure that the slur of those words should come anywhere near her love. So now night after night she must pace up and down, beating her mind against a blind problem, beating her spirit against a blank wall—the impregnable wall of non-comprehension: 'Why am I as I am—and what am I?' Her mind would recoil while her spirit grew faint. A great darkness would seem to descend on her spirit—there would be no light wherewith to lighten that darkness.

She would think of Martin, for now surely she loved just as he had loved—it seemed like madness. She would think of her father, of his comfortable words: 'Don't be foolish, there's nothing strange about you.' Oh, but he must have been pitifully mistaken—he had died still very pitifully mistaken. She would think yet again of her curious childhood, going over each detail in an effort to remember. But after a little her thoughts must plunge forward once more, right into her grievous present. . . . Then would come the most poignant suffering of all, the deepest, the final humiliation. Protection—she could never offer protection to the creature she loved: 'Could you marry me, Stephen?' She could neither protect nor defend nor honour by loving; her hands were completely empty. She who would gladly have given her life, must go empty-handed to love, like a beggar. She could debase what she longed to exalt, defile what she longed to keep pure and untarnished.

The night would gradually change to dawn; and the dawn would shine in at the open windows, bringing with it the intolerable singing of birds: 'Stephen, look at us, look at us, we're happy!' Away in the distance there would be a harsh crying, the wild, harsh crying of swans by the lake—the swan called Peter protecting, defending his mate against some unwelcome intruder. . . . Stephen would fling herself down on the bed, completely exhausted by the night's bitter vigil.[3]

THE PLAY
PICTORIAL

"CAVALCADE"

No. 357

VOL. LIX

Noël Coward &
Radclyffe Hall

1^{s.}
NET

NOEL COWARD

MONTHL

Kindred spirits: a) Coward in 1925 b) "John" around the time she met Coward

Compare the Old Testament gloom here with a Coward lyric from around the same time, "Any Little Fish Can Swim," from *Cochran's 1931 Revue*:

I've fallen in love with you,
I'm taking it badly,
Freezing, burning,
Tossing, turning,
Never know when to laugh or cry,
Just look what our dumb friends do, they welcome it gladly.
Passion in a dromedary doesn't go so deep,
Camels when they're mating never sob themselves to sleep,
Buffaloes can revel in it, so can any sheep;
Why can't I?

Any little fish can swim, any little bird can fly,
Any little dog and any little cat
Can do a bit of this and just a bit of that;
Any little horse can neigh, and any little cow can moo,
But I can't do anything at all
But just love you.

Any little cock can crow, any little fox can run,
Any little crab on any little shore
Can have a little dab and then a little more,
Any little owl can hoot, and any little dove can coo,
But I can't do anything at all
But just love you.

You've pulled me across the brink,
You've chained me and bound me,
No escape now,
Buy the crepe now,
When is the funeral going to be?
Whenever I stop to think,
See nature all around me,

Then I see how stupidly monogamous I am,
A lion in the circumstances wouldn't give a damn,
For if there was no lioness he'd lie down with a lamb;
Why can't I?

Any little bug can bite, any little bee can buzz,
Any little snail on any little oak
Can feel a little frail and have a little joke;
Any little frog can jump like any little kangaroo,
But I can't do anything at all
But just love you.

Any little duck can quack, any little worm can crawl,
Any little mole can frolic in the sun
And make a little hole and have a little fun;
Any little snake can hiss in any little local zoo,
But I can't do anything at all
But just love you.[4]

It helps of course to hear Coward himself singing these lines; he in fact recorded a delightfully silly version of "Any Little Fish" in the 1930s for HMV.[5] The exquisitely mannered falsetto voice, set off by bouncy xylophone accompaniment, makes the absurd little zoological lyric still more ridiculous than it is on the page. But even without benefit of musical performance, the contrast with Hall could hardly be more stark. Both dramatize a state of emotional frustration—a feeling of loving against the grain and being out of sync with a more spontaneous natural order. (The apparent throwaway line in the second verse of the Coward song—"A lion in the circumstances wouldn't give a damn, / For if there was no lioness he'd lie down with a lamb"—invites us to read in, perhaps, the thinly disguised homosexual subtext.) Yet Hall is dejection and woe, Coward gaiety and light; she seems turgid and self-pitying, he remains effervescent and offhand. Out of such binarisms, one suspects, stereotypes are born: lesbians are humorless and self-involved; gay men, worldly and facetious.[6]

One might put the binarism another way: the lesbian is She Who May Be Satirized; the homosexual man He Who Satirizes. Radclyffe Hall has of course been fair game for caricaturists ever since *The Well*'s publication in 1928. A number of parodies and lampoons of the novel appeared in the wake of the celebrated obscenity trial: Henry von Rhau's *The Hell of Loneliness* (1929), P. R. Stephensen's *The Well of Sleevelessness* (1929), even an anonymous mock heroic poem, *The Sink of Solitude* (1928)—complete with Beardsley-esque frontispiece of Hall as a languorous sapphic Christ upon the cross. But mocking portraits crop up in less ephemeral works too: in *Extraordinary Women* (1928), Compton Mackenzie's comic fantasia about lesbian expatriate society on the island of Capri; in Djuna Barnes's *Ladies Almanack* (1928); and in Molly Keane's sardonic novel

of manners, *Devoted Ladies* (1933). Barnes's depiction of Hall and her lover, Una, Lady Troubridge, as the dog-loving, monocle-sporting "Tilly-Tweed-in-Blood" and "Lady Buck-and-Balk" exasperated Hall; even some of her fellow inverts were among the caricaturists. In a 1983 afterword to her early novel *The Friendly Young Ladies* (1944), the lesbian novelist Mary Renault described reading the then-banned *Well of Loneliness* aloud with a friend in France in the 1930s and being unable to keep from falling into "rather heartless laughter":

> It had been out for ten years, which is a long time in terms of the conventions; but it does, I still think, carry an impermissible allowance of self-pity, and its earnest humourlessness invites irreverence. Solemn, dead-pan descriptions of Mary [Stephen's first lover] knitting stockings for Stephen—and when there was real silk!—and mending her "masculine underwear" (what can it have been! It was long before briefs; perhaps Wolsey combinations) are passages I can still not read with entire gravity.[7]

Renault recognized Hall as a powerful cultural icon—a self-appointed mascot of the lesbian cause—yet one to be resisted and rejected. ("People who do not consider themselves to be, primarily, human beings among their fellow-humans, deserve to be discriminated against, and ought not to make a meal of it.")[8] And indeed *The Friendly Young Ladies*, with its wry send-up of Freud and the glum sexological theories of homosexuality so dear to Hall and her circle, might be considered yet another comic rewriting of *The Well*.[9]

It's almost impossible to imagine satirizing Coward, if only because he was himself one of the master satirists of his era. Starting with his first work, the ludicrous unfinished novel *Cherry Pan* (1918), verbal assault on pretension and bathos was a favorite Coward mode. ("Cherry Pan," he wrote later in a retrospective of his career, "was the daughter of the Great God Pan and was garrulous and tiresome to the point of nausea. Having materialized suddenly on a summer evening in Sussex, she proceeded with excruciating pagan archness to wreak havoc in a country parsonage before returning winsomely to her woodland glades and elfin grots. I remember being bitterly offended by a friend who suggested that the title should be changed to *Bedpan*."[10])

Coward was an accomplished if broad literary parodist: the burlesque portrait of Edith Sitwell as "Hernia Whittlebot" in *London Calling* (1922–23) and *Chelsea Buns* (1924)—"she scatters the tepid tea-leaves of Victorian Aspiration and Georgian achievement with the incisive *mesquinerie* of a literary Bonaparte"—is still surprisingly funny after seventy years; so are the simpering specimens of modernist verse, by "Crispin Pither," "Juana Mandragagita," "Janet Urdler," and other supposed poetical luminaries, in *Spangled Unicorn* (1932).[11] Coward was a master of the post-Wildean epigram: asked in a 1960s television interview if he believed in God, he replied, "We've never been intimate, but I think perhaps we have a few things in common."[12] Coward's whole career might be considered an "improved" version of Wilde's—a Wildean life without the final, unhinging tragedy. Coward's best plays—*Private Lives, Design for Living*—come close to rivaling Wilde's in wit and intellectual compass, yet he entirely lacked Wilde's curious, soiling streak of self-destructiveness. By making light—to the very end—Coward kept it light.[13]

And yet, as is often the way with apparent opposites—especially when human beings are involved—the contrast between Noël Coward and Radclyffe Hall is perhaps more presumptive than real. It comes as something of a shock, first of all, to discover that the two writers knew each other—and knew each other well—through a large interlocking network of shared literary and theatrical friends and acquaintances. Coward and Hall were part of the same homosexual and artistic "smart set" active in London, Paris, and New York in the early 1920s; later in the decade, when many gay and lesbian bohemians began gravitating to the Kent and Sussex countryside, they lived within a few miles of each other—Hall at Rye on the Sussex coast and Coward at Goldenhurst near Aldington.

But social connections were not the only connections. For more than twenty years a kind of subtle imaginative cross-fertilization took place between them. Each produced "ghostly" fictional portraits of the other: Hall modeled the most interesting (if also most problematic) male character in *The Well of Loneliness* on Coward; Coward's works of the 1920s, '30s, and '40s (Hall died in 1943) contain a number of disguised portraits of Hall. And each was given, if surreptitiously, to a kind of literary "gesturing" toward the other. (The most elaborate of these private tributes is undoubtedly Coward's ironic reworking of Hall's eccentric love life in the mordant 1941 domestic farce *Blithe Spirit*.) However covertly or incongruously, "Radclyffe Hall" inhabits the work of Noël Coward, and "Noël Coward" the work of Radclyffe Hall.

The connection between Hall and Coward has not been examined; biographers mention their friendship, if at all, only in passing.[14] Somehow one is not surprised: exploring the link between them confounds the symbolic opposition that seems so powerfully to divide male and female homosexuals in the popular imagination. For the past forty or fifty years, but especially since Stonewall, our perceptions of the gay and lesbian past have been deeply shaped—too deeply shaped—by intellectual separatism: by the assumption that male and female homosexual cliques have little to do with one another and represent different subcultural traditions. This will to segregate has come from both the right and the left. On one side of the spectrum are those who believe that only homosexual men are interesting and worth bothering about—*tout court*. "Male homosexuality," writes Camille Paglia in a recent essay on sexuality and the avant-garde, "pushing outward into risky, alien territory, is progressive and, overall, intellectually stimulating. Lesbianism, seeking a lost state of blissful union with the mother, is cozy, regressive, and I'm sorry to say, too often intellectually enervating, tending toward the inert."[15] Hence one misogynistic rationale for segregation: since lesbians never do anything but hanker after Mummy, it is safe to assume they have had little to do, historically speaking, with the real architects of civilization—gay men.[16]

In turn, those who want to correct for such bias have often overcompensated. While well meaning in the abstract, the post-Stonewall lesbian-feminist search for an authentic "lesbian tradition" or "lesbian imagination"—a distinct history of achievement, say, in literature or the arts—has frequently led to misunderstanding the real-world contexts in which lesbian artists and writers have flourished. Lesbian creativity is presumed to take place within its own closed sphere; links between lesbian writers and artists and their male contemporaries have been unnecessarily obscured. Thus much will be made of Willa Cather's debt to Sarah Orne Jewett, for example, or Renée Vivien's to Natalie Barney but not of Cather's debt to Henry James or Vivien's to Baudelaire and Verlaine. Lesbian writers end up insulated and marginalized, while one's overall picture of literary history remains largely unchanged.

Yet the history of homosexual creativity in the nineteenth and twentieth centuries is full of vibrant cross-gender relationships. What one might call emotional bisexuality—often involving some sort of creative "marriage" or symbolic siblinghood with a homosexual person of the opposite sex—has been a central part of gay and lesbian experience.[17] In some cases, of course, real marriage has been part of the equation: witness the well-known (and more or less expedient) unions of Vita Sackville-West and Harold Nicolson, Bryher and Robert McAlmon, Somerset and Syrie Maugham, Paul and Jane Bowles, or W. H. Auden and Erika Mann. But even without official ties, gay men and lesbians have constantly formed enabling bonds. We need a history of cross-sex homosexual sociability that will take into account such diverse creative "couples" as Henry James and Constance Fenimore Woolson, Walter Pater and Vernon Lee, Virginia Woolf and E. M. Forster, Lytton Strachey and Dora Carrington, Ethel Smyth and E. F. Benson, Gertrude Stein and Virgil Thomson, Cole Porter and Elsie de Wolfe, Nella Larsen and Carl Van Vechten, Greta Garbo and Cecil Beaton, Dorothy Strachey and André Gide, Djuna Barnes and Dan Mahoney (the model for the oracular Matthew "Mighty" O'Connor in Barnes's *Nightwood*), Sylvia Townsend Warner and T. H. White, Janet Flanner and Tennessee Williams, Violet Trefusis and Francis Poulenc, Natalie Barney and Jean Cocteau, Violette Leduc and Maurice Sachs, Marguerite

Yourcenar and Jerry Wilson, Elizabeth Bishop and James Merrill, and countless others.[18]

In foregrounding the relationship between Coward and Hall, I thus embark on an emblematic endeavor: to make each of them, "Noël Coward" and "Radclyffe Hall," seem less uniform, less easy to categorize, less the prisoner of a particular biographical or ideological stereotype. But in bringing their forgotten relationship into the open, I also want to call attention to the larger historical links between gay male and lesbian culture in the twentieth century. The intellectual, emotional, and spiritual bonding between homosexual men and women is one of civilization's more engaging love stories and deserves at some point to be fully told. Let the following "double portrait" of Noël Coward and Radclyffe Hall serve as notes toward that story.

First, a reconstruction. It is difficult to date Hall and Coward's first meeting exactly, but they almost certainly encountered one another late in 1923 or early 1924, at the height of Coward's first theatrical success. The twenty-three-year-old Coward was already acclaimed as a playwright and actor: he had written and starred in the hit comedies *I'll Leave it to You* (1920) and *The Young Idea* (1923), collaborated with Ronald Jeans on the wildly popular musical revue *London Calling!* (1923), and was on the verge of even greater stardom. His scandalous "problem" drama of 1924, *The Vortex*, in which he gave an over-the-top performance as the jazz-playing, mother-obsessed, drug-addicted hero, Nicky Lancaster, would make him, along with Ivor Novello, the most famous (and most photographed) British stage actor of the day, both in London and New York. Throughout the early '20s he was regularly featured in the London weeklies and entertainment papers: a picture of him wearing silk pajamas, talking on the telephone, and eating breakfast in bed ("Noël the Fortunate: The Young Playwright, Actor, and Composer, Mr. Noël Coward, Busy at Breakfast") on the cover of *The Sketch* in April 1925 did much to fix his popular image as the embodiment of glamorous, dissipated, slightly shocking '20s chic. "I was seldom mentioned in the press," he wrote later, "without allusions to cocktails, decadence and post-war hysteria."[19] Nonetheless—hysteria notwithstanding—"success took me to her bosom like a maternal boa constrictor."[20]

Hall—though a late bloomer—was also coming into her own in the early '20s. By 1923, after publishing several books of poetry, she started writing novels; her first, *The Forge*, appeared in 1924 to excellent notices. She followed with *The Unlit Lamp* later that year, *A Saturday Life* in 1925, and the best-selling *Adam's Breed*—winner of both the Prix Femina and the prestigious James Tait Black prize—in 1926. Her private life, which had gone through some upheavals in the teens, was also relatively calm. She regarded her relationship with Una Troubridge, her lover of eight years, as a marriage—and indeed it was, though of an unconventional sort.

When they met in 1915, Troubridge was married to a high-ranking admiral (from whom she later separated) and Hall was the lover of Edwardian society matron and fashionable salon singer Mabel ("Ladye") Batten. Hall and Troubridge embarked on a passionate clandestine affair, only to be found out by Batten, who died, broken-hearted, of a stroke in 1916. Stricken with guilt, the two lovers—both of whom were fascinated by the occult—began seeing a well-known medium, Mrs. Osborne Leonard, in the hope of contacting Batten. After "Ladye" sent conciliatory messages from beyond the grave, Hall and Troubridge, overwhelmed with relief, began having regular weekly "communica-

The youthful prodigy:
a) "Noel the Fortunate" on the
cover of *The Sketch*, 1924
b) still fortunate in 1927

tions" with her through Mrs. Leonard. These sessions, which seem to have functioned for them as therapy or marriage counseling, continued for many years. In December 1919 they published a 215-page article (with lesbian details suppressed) about their experiences in the *Proceedings of the Society for Psychical Research* and were immediately taken up by several prominent spiritualists, including the distinguished scientist Sir Oliver Lodge. They became enthusiastic converts to the spiritualist cause. When Hall published *The Well of Loneliness* in 1928, she dedicated it to "Our Three Selves," in cryptic allusion to the curious relationship between herself, Troubridge, and "Ladye."

Hall in black sombrero and cape from
Nathan's theatrical *costumier,* 1920

With Hall's public reputation as a writer growing (she was elected to PEN in 1922), she and Troubridge—both of whom had independent fortunes—began moving in fashionable London society. From 1922 on, they appeared frequently at literary gatherings, theatrical parties, and first nights—often in the company of lesbian actress friends and acquaintances such as Teddie Gerard and Tallulah Bankhead. Hall's biographer Michael Baker writes of this hectic "first night" phase: "She and Una sometimes attended as many as three or four different plays a week, matinees as well as evenings. Because they knew several successful actresses, this ritual was partly a service to friends. But the 'first night' in the Twenties was also a great social occasion, an opportunity to see and be seen.

The hectic years: Hall and Troubridge at the first night of *When Ladies Meet,* 1933

Graphic resemblances:
a) Coward
(with Gertrude Lawrence)
b) Hall seen by cartoonists
"Pax" and "Matt," after she
won the James Tait Black
Prize for *Adam's Breed,* 1926

MISS RADCLIFFE HALL.
(who has been awarded the Femina Prize for
her book "Adam's Breed").
"' At home on Pegasus, that valiant steed ;
Yet finds romance in Soho'—' Adam's Breed.'"

Miss Radclyffe Hall
From a caricature by Matt

Though John [the name Hall commonly went by to friends] was a shy, diffident person, she enjoyed the limelight of this particular arena." Hall had her hair cut short and shingled in 1920 and liked to dress for such occasions in flamboyant, androgynous sombreros and cloaks purchased at Nathan's theatrical costumier. "At a time when theatre-goers commonly dressed in evening clothes," Baker observes, "John's appearance in high stiff collar, man's stock, and black military cloak invariably caused a stir. The romantic actor in her thrived on this attention and, with her customary style, she rarely disappointed expectations."[21] Photographs and caricatures of "the noted author, Miss Radclyffe Hall" began to appear with some regularity in magazines like *T.P.'s Weekly* and *Popular Pictorial*. By 1928, according to the *Manchester Despatch*, she was "the most easily-recognized artistic celebrity in London."[22]

Mutual friends: a) Gabrielle Enthoven, founder of the Theatre Museum b) the American revue actress Teddie Gerard

Hall and Coward met through shared friends in the theater—probably the playwright Gabrielle Enthoven or the American singer-actress Teddie Gerard. Gabrielle Enthoven, an old acquaintance of Mabel "Ladye" Batten's who had adapted D'Annunzio's *The Honeysuckle* for the stage, was an important mutual friend: she met Coward in 1921 during his first visit to New York, when he stayed with her and her lover Cecile Sartoris in Greenwich Village. (Sartoris made a precarious living by reciting Verlaine poems in the homes of the wealthy, accompanied by the husky-voiced Polish chanteuse "Poldowski," Irene Dean-Paul, daughter of the composer Wieniawski. Poldowski may be one of the models for Wanda, the alcoholic artist in *The Well of Loneliness* who sings Polish love songs in a "heavy contralto voice.") Enthoven already knew Hall and Troubridge well, and when Enthoven returned to London in 1923, she introduced them at once to the Coward theatrical set and possibly to Coward himself. The three women were often seen together in 1923 and 1924 at the popular actors' nightclub, the Cave of Harmony in Charlotte Street, and the Orange Tree Club, one of several private Soho clubs of the '20s at which homosexuals were allowed to dance together.[23]

The revue actress Teddie Gerard was an even closer connection. Coward had known her since the teens; Hall met her in June 1923, after Gerard began making a name for herself in various "naughty" London musicals. (She was the first actress to sport backless evening gowns and was accompanied on stage by a line of male choristers who sang "Glad to See You're Back, Dear Lady."[24]) The following winter, Gerard replaced Coward's leading lady, Gertrude Lawrence, in the extended run of *London Calling!* If Hall and Coward had not already met through Gabrielle Enthoven, they were almost certainly introduced by Gerard in the winter of 1923–24. The hard-drinking, extroverted Gerard was one of Hall and Trou-

Coward and Tallulah Bankhead, during the run of *Fallen Angels,* 1925

bridge's closest friends at the time, and the three of them, along with Gerard's lover Etheline, made frequent parties backstage and at Gerard's flat in Sackville Street. Hall and Troubridge were also regular weekend guests at Gerard's house in the country, both before and after the stint in *London Calling!*[25]

By the mid-twenties Hall and Coward shared a host of literary and theatrical friends: the sultry-voiced Tallulah Bankhead (Bankhead met Hall in 1924 and starred in the London production of Coward's *Fallen Angels* in 1925), the actor Ernest Thesiger, the novelists Michael Arlen and Sheila Kaye-Smith, the critic James Agate, the sewing-machine heiress Winnaretta Singer (Comtesse de Polignac), and the novelist and playwright Clemence Dane (Winifred Ashton), whose discreetly lesbian-themed novel, *Regiment of Women*, had appeared in 1917. (It was Dane, later one of Coward's closest female friends, whom Hall approached in 1929 when she was

Hall and Troubridge's signatures in Coward's Goldenhurst guestbook, September 13, 1928, during the outcry over *The Well of Loneliness*

seeking a playwright to dramatize *The Well of Loneliness* for the London stage. Dane refused, on the ground that *The Well* was not suitable for theatrical adaptation.) Later on, in 1930, Hall and Troubridge became acquainted with the strikingly attractive Gladys Calthrop—former lover of Eva Le Gallienne and Coward's designer and artistic collaborator throughout the '20s and '30s.

But the connection with Coward himself was a strong one and from 1926 on can be documented more directly. After Coward bought a country house, Goldenhurst, in the Romney Marsh region in Kent—an area known as a mecca for gay and lesbian bohemians since the 1890s—Hall and Troubridge were among the many London friends he invited down.[26] Their signatures first appear in the Goldenhurst guest book on September 13, 1928—at the height of the public furor over *The Well of Loneliness*. Despite the fact that Coward took no public stand on the book—he was not among the forty or so writers and public figures to sign on as defense witnesses when the book was brought to trial for obscenity in November—he evidently provided Hall with much-needed behind-the-scenes moral support.[27] The two women returned his hospitality. After Hall and Troubridge purchased the Black Boy, a restored fourteenth-century house in nearby Rye, Coward was a regular dinner guest.* Both admired his wit and charm and professional savoir faire. (He was their first choice for the lead in Troubridge's stage adaptation of Colette's *Chéri* in 1930.) At one dinner party in 1930, Coward told so many hilarious stories, wrote Troubridge in her diary, that the Black Boy rang with "howls" of laughter. Coward, she observed, was "one of the only people I know who succeeds in being chronically and excruciatingly witty without victimising anyone."[28]

If nothing else, the numerous social links between Hall and Coward give the lie to the view, sometimes still bruited, that male and female homosexual subcultures of the early twentieth century should be studied in isolation from each other. In an otherwise illuminating recent essay on Coward and the "politics of homosexual representation" in the English theater before 1950, the gay scholar Alan Sinfield argues, somewhat confusingly, that because theater and "illicit [male] sexual activity" are likely to occupy the same "inner-city territory," one need not bother trying to seek out connections between lesbians and male homosexual playwrights like Coward:

*Like Coward, Hall and Troubridge may have been attracted to England's southeast coast in part because of its many literary (and homosexual) associations. Henry James, Ford Madox Ford, Stephen Crane, Joseph Conrad, and H. G. Wells had all lived in the Romney Marsh region in the early part of the century; Rye, especially, by the 1920s had become a literary-bohemian mecca. Between 1919 and 1940 the comic novelist E. F. Benson lived in James's former home, Lamb House, just down the High Street from Hall and Troubridge, who met him in 1930; his famous series of comic novels featuring Miss Mapp and Lucia (*Queen Lucia*, *Mapp and Lucia*, *Trouble for Lucia*, and so on) presents a vivid picture of Rye's gay and lesbian coterie. Other friends and acquaintances in the vicinity included the homosexual writer Francis Yeats-Brown, author of *Bengal Lancers* (1930); Lady Maud Warrender, one-time mayoress of Rye, who lived with the singer Marcia van Dresser; the former suffragette commandant Mary ("Robert") Allen; and the curious lesbian threesome, Christopher St. John, Clare ("Tony") Atwood, and Edy Craig (daughter of Ellen Terry and model for Miss La Trobe in Virginia Woolf's *Between the Acts*), who lived together at Smallhythe and appear in many memoirs from the period. See Iain Finlayson, *The Sixth Continent: A Literary History of Romney Marsh* (New York: Atheneum, 1986), Brian Masters, *E. F. Benson* (London: Chatto & Windus, 1991), and Joy Melville, *Ellen and Edy: A Biography of Ellen Terry and Her Daughter, Edith Craig, 1847–1947* (London and New York: Pandora, 1987).

Since the late nineteenth century, theater bars and adjacent public houses and coffee bars in London's West End have been known as meeting places [for homosexual men]. I resist the idea of an intrinsic link between homosexuality and theater, since I believe neither to be essentially thus or thus, but both to be contingent, cultural phenomena—subject to the pressures and limits of a specific historical moment and figuring differently in different parts of the social order. For this reason I hardly include lesbians in the present discussion: though their history has had a certain amount in common with that of male homosexuals, it has also been quite distinct.[29]

Sinfield's failure here to see lesbians as playing any significant part in the history of "homosexual representation"—at least with regard to British theater—results in some dubious historical claims: the assertion, for example, that Mordaunt Shairp's play *The Green Bay Tree* (1933) "was the most explicit play [on homosexuality] permitted in a public theater until *A Taste of Honey* in 1958." (An English-language adaptation of Christa Winsloe's lesbian-themed Berlin stage hit, *Mädchen in Uniform*, starring Jessica Tandy and Cathleen Nesbitt, played in London in 1932.[30]) But Sinfield also ends up giving a lop-sided impression of the artistic milieu in which Coward lived and worked. Like Cole Porter's, Coward's career cannot be understood solely as the expression of a male homosexual aesthetic.[31] He had scores of women friends and actively supported the careers of many; more important, almost all his closest professional associates were either lesbian or bisexual, including his secretary-manager Lorn Loraine and his designer Gladys Calthrop.

Coward worked with numerous lesbian-identified actresses, writers, and directors: Gabrielle Enthoven, Teddie Gerard, Tallulah Bankhead, Mercedes de Acosta, Blyth Daly, Eva Le Gallienne, Katharine Cornell, Clemence Dane, Estelle Winwood, Elsa Maxwell, Beatrice Lillie, Marlene Dietrich, Mary Martin. Even his most celebrated leading lady, Gertrude Lawrence, was discreetly bisexual: she had a passionate affair with Daphne du Maurier in the 1940s. (Du Maurier fell in love with the charismatic "Gertie," she later confessed, in 1930 while watching her play Amanda in *Private Lives*.[32]) Indeed, so ubiquitous were Coward's lesbian friendships, one is tempted to pronounce him, like Cole Porter or Carl Van Vechten or Cecil Beaton, a kind of "male lesbian"—a man so responsive to female homosexuality, so psychically *involved* in its recognition, that conventional sexual categories seem ill adapted to describe him.[33]

Before turning to specific artistic affiliations between Coward and Hall, let me conclude this section by symbolizing their forgotten connection—and the cultural bond between 1920s gay men and lesbians generally—with a series of images from the period. Coward expressed his attraction to lesbian women visually—by appearing with astonishing frequency in publicity photographs with his lesbian or bisexual collaborators. Perhaps more than any other male star of the epoch he seems to have relished representing himself as part of a creative duo, as having a female (usually homosexual) counterpart or alter ego. His fondness for what one might call the "binary portrait" bears this out. By binary portrait—the term is my own invention—I mean a type of fashionable formal portrait, loosely art deco in inspiration, with two sitters posing as mirror opposites or as a pair of overlapping, almost identical, profiles. The three images reproduced here illustrate the mode. The first photograph, from 1924, showing Coward back to back with Gladys Calthrop, represents what I am calling the "symmetrical" binary portrait. The second, also from the mid-twenties, with Coward and Calthrop both in profile and facing in the same direction, is an "overlapping" binary portrait. The third, a famous publicity shot from 1930 of Coward and Gertrude Lawrence as Elyot and

Binary portraiture:
a) Coward and designer Gladys Calthrop,
back to back, 1924
b) Coward and Calthrop with matching
profiles, mid-1920s
c) Coward and Gertrude Lawrence in
Private Lives, 1930

Amanda in *Private Lives*—tilted cigarette holders at the ready—is another example of the "symmetrical" binary portrait.

Much might be said, of course, about the binary portrait as a manifestation of '20s and '30s sexual style, which so often turned upon an implicitly "homosexual" confounding of traditional sex roles. Unlike more conventional double portraiture, such as the standard heterosexual marriage portrait in which the husband stands behind his seated or otherwise visually subordinated spouse, the binary portrait emphasizes the sameness and equality of the two individuals portrayed. Sexual differences, including power differences, seem to be blurred or undone; masculinity and femininity lose their emotional outlines. Men and women meet on the same plane, as affectionate comrades or androgynous reflections. In the photo of Coward and Lawrence, for example—or, even more strikingly, in

The third sex: René Vincent's ad for Porto
Ramos-Pinto, 1929

**PORTO
RAMOS-PINTO**

ADRIANO RAMOS PINTO & IRMÃO LDA-PORTO

René Vincent's gorgeous 1929 lithograph advertisement for Porto
Ramos-Pinto—the mirror relationship of the sitters functions as a
visual challenge to heterosexual norms. In Vincent's plate, the two
about-to-kiss figures in black look far more like those "intermediate
types" or members of the "third sex" identified by Edward Carpenter, Havelock Ellis, and other turn-of-the-century sexologists as types
of the homosexual, than like traditional men and women.[34]

Coward was undoubtedly aware on some level of the binary
portrait's gender-blurring possibilities. "Elyot and Amanda are
practically synonymous," he said of the husband and wife protago-
nists of *Private Lives*; playing Elyot to Lawrence's Amanda, he wrote

Lesbian binary portraiture: a) The "YouWe picture": Gluck's *Medallion,* 1937
b) Hall and Troubridge by Jack Seymour
c) Gladys Calthrop self-portait with shadow, ca. 1930

nists of *Private Lives*; playing Elyot to Lawrence's Amanda, he wrote in his memoirs, was like sharing the same part.[35]

Stage pictures of him with Lawrence simply reinforce the point. Yet the various binary portraits for which he posed with Calthrop and Lawrence (and later Marlene Dietrich and Mary Martin) might also be considered coded symbolic tributes: expressions of fellow feeling, emotional identification, and love—the love of the homosexual man for a female kindred spirit. In the Calthrop photos especially, one has the sense of a new sort of male-female connection being celebrated: a creative marriage of male and female homosexual sensibilities.

That sophisticated lesbians recognized Coward's implicit tribute to them would seem to be borne out by numerous lesbian "adaptations" of the binary portrait in the later '20s and '30s. What Coward made fashionable, female couples like Radclyffe Hall and Una Troubridge borrowed for their own expressive purposes. The lesbian artist Gluck's 1937 painting *Medallion*, a double portrait of herself and her lover Nesta Obermer, duplicates almost exactly the pose of Coward and Calthrop in their overlapping portrait of 1924. (Gluck called her painting the "YouWe" picture and wrote to Obermer after completing it: "There never has been such a thing as Us. . . . Darling Heart, we are not an 'affair' are we—We are husband and wife."[36]) A binary portrait in oils of Hall and Troubridge by Jack Seymour may be another oblique homage.[37]

Yet Radclyffe Hall's response to Coward's self-fashioning may have run deeper. Comparing pictures of them from the '20s, one can hardly miss the physiognomic and sartorial similarities. That one or both (though most probably Hall) sought to accentuate the likeness is a distinct possibility. At any rate, photographs make it clear that both were intensely concerned with matters of clothing, hair, and personal style.* Coward especially, like the Prince of Wales after him, was a renowned sartorial trendsetter. "Coward's sense of personal style," Robert F. Kiernan writes, "shaped not only the theatrical stage but the stage of life":

> His exaggeratedly clipped speech and his breezily insouciant manner were imitated both onstage and off. . . . Coward's manner of calling the most solemn endeavors "lots of fun" and of peppering every sentence with the adjective [sic] "terribly" became endemic in fashionable speech, and all sorts of men transformed themselves into Noël Coward look-alikes, slick and satiny. . . . His wearing of crewneck pullovers was much imitated after his success in *The Vortex*, and his sumptuous dressing gowns worn over trousers, shirt, and tie became acceptable attire in drawing rooms. His bow ties, his brown dinner-jacket suits, and the white silk scarves he affected with navy blue casual clothes had immeasurable influence among the sartorially conscious.[38]

Was Hall—whose studious cultivation of the same "slick and satiny" masculine look throughout the '20s made her famous—one of Coward's many imitators? Her biographer Michael Baker notes that Hall cut her hair in a mannish style in 1920, the same year she began wearing the brocade smoking jackets and bow ties in which she later posed for studio portraits. At the time of the *Well* trial in 1928 a reporter for the *New York Telegram Magazine* described her:

*Coward wrote of the changes in his wardrobe after the overnight success of *The Vortex*:

> I indulged immediately a long-suppressed desire for silk shirts, pyjamas and underclothes. I opened up accounts at various shops, happy to be able to charge things without that inward fear that I might never be able to pay for them. I wasted a lot of money this way, but it was worth it. My clothes certainly began to improve, but I was still inclined to ruin a correct ensemble by some flashy error of taste.

And elsewhere:

> I took to wearing coloured turtle-necked jerseys, actually more for comfort than for effect, and soon I was informed by my evening paper that I had started a fashion. I believe that to a certain extent this was really true; at any rate, during the ensuing months I noticed more and more of our seedier West End chorus boys parading about London in them. See Coward, *Present Indicative*, pp. 198 and 204.

The Coward style:
a) in the famous dressing gown, with
Lillian Braithwaite in *The Vortex*, 1924
b) in *We Were Dancing*, 1936

She is Byronese in appearance and friends call her "John." Her jewels, large emeralds sunk in rings of platinum, are the only softening note in her mannish profile.

Her features are sensitive, her eyes sad with the loneliness of a little girl not asked to the party. Her short blond hair is combed straight back and her blue shirt is Bond Street tailored. Her shirt is blue linen with a standing collar and the tie navy. She wears a monocle on a cord, a watch in her handkerchief pocket suspended on a leather fob from the lapel button-hole. In the evening Miss Hall wears a moire tuxedo with a satin stock and a ruffled shirt front. Her hat is a large Montmartre similar to our broad-brimmed "Westerners."[39]

In a sense Hall was in advance of the Coward vogue, which developed after the success of *The Vortex* in 1924. Like Gluck, Greta Garbo, and the poet-screenwriter Mercedes de Acosta, Hall was a pioneer of what might be called the "high style" in lesbian fashion between the wars.[40] Yet as she moved toward an increasingly sleek, androgynous look in the later '20s, the Coward influence became unmistakable. Hall shared Coward's fascination with unusual dinner jackets, Chinese silk, and fancy haberdashery, as well as his matinee-idol penchant for being photographed, glamorous and unsmiling, with cigarette in hand. (She gives similar tastes to the heroine of *The Well*: Stephen Gordon favors "pyjamas made of white crepe de Chine" and buys "a man's dressing-gown of brocade—an amazingly ornate garment" while shopping for presents for Angela Crossby on Bond Street.) Indeed, despite being short, almost twenty years older, and of a different sex, Radclyffe Hall managed to create a remarkably faithful imitation of the svelte Coward silhouette. The effect was sometimes heightened, or so photographs of her with Troubridge suggest, by her companion's appearance: Troubridge's carefully bobbed and waved hair, an epitome of '20s feminine chic, was often strikingly reminiscent of Gertrude Lawrence's.

The evolution of lesbian high style:
a) Radclyffe Hall as debutante, ca. 1900
b) in bow tie, 1921
c) as budding seductress, 1926
d) as "Byronese" hero, 1928
e) as matinee idol, 1932

35

The competition: a) the painter
Gluck in 1926 by E. A. Hoppé
b) poet and screenwriter
Mercedes de Acosta, 1934

It would be nice to pause here over a photograph of Coward and Hall together—if not a formal binary portrait, then a simple snapshot of the sort that turn up in memoirs and evocations of the era. If only we had something like the wonderfully louche photo from the 1950s—reproduced in the picture album *Noël Coward and His Friends* (1979)—of Coward sunbathing in the nude with Katharine Cornell and her companion Nancy Hamilton, Cornell's homosexual husband Guthrie McLintic, and Coward's lover Graham Payn. One could hardly wish for a more exquisite, if risible, emblem of gay and lesbian solidarity. In the absence of such an image, however—comic or otherwise—let us turn to the writing that Hall and Coward produced. For here, after all, their relationship is perhaps

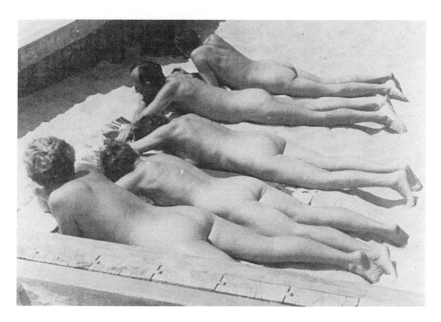

Gay and lesbian history in the buff: Nancy Hamilton, Katharine Cornell, Guthrie McLintic, Noel Coward, and Graham Payn, ca. 1950

most fully laid bare: not in the momentary revelation of the camera flash but in the more durable realm of the imagination.

That was the worst of Jonathan Brockett, he could make you laugh in spite of yourself—when you most disapproved you found yourself laughing.

—*Radclyffe Hall,* The Well of Loneliness, *1928*[41]

We may not always find ourselves laughing with Jonathan Brockett—though ebullient, he is ultimately powerless against *The Well*'s great melancholic downward swirl—but he does represent a crucial, temporary, lightening of mood: an element of chiaroscuro in the novel's overall somber pattern.

At quarter-past eight he arrived, late for dinner and loaded like a pack-mule with brown paper parcels. He looked cross; he had spoilt his new reindeer gloves with mayonnaise that had oozed through a box containing the lobster salad.

He thrust the box into Stephen's hands. 'Here, you take it—it's dripping. Can I have a wash rag?' but after a moment he forgot the new gloves. 'I've raided Fortnum and Mason—such fun—I do *love* eating things out of cardboard boxes. Hallo, Puddle darling! I sent you a plant. Did you get it? A nice little plant with brown bobbles. It smells good, and it's got a ridiculous name like an old Italian dowager or something. Wait a minute—what's it called? Oh, yes, a baronia—it's so humble to have such a pompous name! Stephen, do be careful—don't rock the lobster about like that. I told you the thing was dripping!'

'I want lots and lots of dishes,' he announced. Then unfortunately he happened to notice the parlourmaid's washing, just back from the laundry.

'Brockett, what on earth are you doing?'

He had put on the girl's ornate frilled cap, and was busily tying on her small apron. He paused for a moment. 'How do I look? What a perfect duck of an apron!' (228–29)

Is Brockett Coward? Or Hall's version of Coward? Hall often modeled fictional characters on living individuals: some of the matchups in *The Well* are close enough to suggest the roman à clef. Valérie Seymour, the sophisticated lesbian hostess who takes Stephen under her wing in Paris after Stephen leaves home, is patently modeled on the charismatic Natalie Barney, whose salon on the Rue Jacob was a haven for lesbian writers and artists between the wars. Along with her lover, the painter Romaine Brooks, Barney became one of Hall and Troubridge's good friends in the 1920s. Other characters, especially those who appear in the Paris chapters, resemble homosexual men and women Hall knew on both sides of the channel in the postwar years— Mimi Franchetti, Adrien Mirtil, Violette Murat, Ida Rubinstein, and Lily de Gramont, the Duchesse de Clermont-Tonnerre.[42] Hall often borrowed physical details directly: Valérie Seymour, like her real-life prototype Barney, has "very blue, very lustrous" eyes and "masses of thick fair hair, which was busily ridding itself of its hairpins; one could see at a glance that it hated restraint" (244).

Certain details link Jonathan Brockett with Coward from the start. Brockett is a fashionable London playwright, with stage successes that take him, intermittently, to New York and Paris. He and the heroine, Stephen, meet midway through the novel at an "old-fashioned, Kensington luncheon party," where he succeeds, by dint of wit and persistence, in drawing the awkward young woman into conversation. (Stephen, exiled from friends and family after a painful botched love affair, has just published her first successful novel.)

Coward with Gerald du Maurier at a theatrical garden party in the late 1920s

Brockett was a connection of the Carringtons; had he not been
Stephen might never have met him, for such gatherings bored him
exceedingly, and therefore it was not his habit to attend them. But on
that occasion he had not been bored, for his sharp, grey eyes had lit
upon Stephen; and as soon as he could, he had made his way to her
side and had remained there. She had found him exceedingly easy to
talk to, as indeed he had wished her to find him. (226)

The physical resemblance to Coward is strong—even down to
the insinuating "feminine" hands:

Stephen was never able to decide whether Jonathan Brockett
attracted or repelled her. Brilliant he could be at certain times, yet
curiously foolish and puerile at others; and his hands were as white
and soft as a woman's—she would feel a queer little sense of out-

41

Caricatures of Coward by Autori, 1920s

rage creeping over her when she looked at his hands. For those hands of his went so ill with him somehow; he was tall, broad-shouldered, and of an extreme thinness. His clean-shaven face was slightly sardonic and almost disconcertingly clever; an inquisitive face too—one felt that it pried into everyone's secrets without shame or mercy. (226)

Coward's white hands, languidly supporting a cigarette, were of course an essential part of his visual mystique—and "womanly" enough to make his occasional drag appearances fairly unnerving. (Witness the photo of him with Gerald du Maurier at a theatrical costume party in the late '20s.) Later in the novel, after Brockett returns from war service in the Mediterranean—Coward served briefly in the Artists' Rifles in 1918—Stephen notes the "little bags" of flesh "showing under his eyes" and "rather deep lines at the sides of his mouth." Coward's face was marked by both—the eye pouches would become increasingly puffy and pronounced with age—so much so that contemporary caricaturists were wont to use them as defining or signature physiognomic details.[43]

But other details secure a connection. In presenting Brockett as the novel's truth teller and emotional guide—a homosexual Virgil to Stephen's lesbian Dante—Hall reinforces the Coward link. Brockett, Stephen realizes with some uneasiness after meeting him, "glues his eyes to other people's keyholes" in order to write his "fiendishly clever" plays. ("That was why Brockett wrote such fine plays, such cruel plays; he fed his genius on live flesh and blood" [234]). Coward too peered through keyholes. As a dramatist he delighted in exposing his characters' most embarrassing secrets and challenging bourgeois pieties in the process. *The Vortex*, which concluded with the sensational revelation of the hero's drug habit and half-incestuous love for his mother, was the first demonstration of this provocative side to Coward's art, but several other early Coward plays—as reviewers such as James Agate were quick to notice—had their Ibsenesque moments.

Fallen Angels, besides dealing with adultery and sexual jealousy, suggested emotional complexities between its two female characters (played by Tallulah Bankhead and Edna Best) far exceeding conventional theatrical expectations; even farces like *Hay Fever*—for all the surface insouciance—had a subversive undertow that some playgoers found disquieting. (One critic wrote, "There is neither health nor cleanness about any of Mr. Coward's characters, who are still the same vicious babies sprawling on the floor of their unwholesome crèche."[44]) Around the time that Hall was composing *The Well* (1926–27), Coward wrote—while correctly surmising he would never get it produced—a dark comedy entitled *Semi-Monde*, featuring several explicitly lesbian and gay characters. This work—to which I will return later—has certain thematic affiliations with *The Well*.

Not surprisingly, with his "hard clever face" and eye pressed sharply "to that secret keyhole," Jonathan Brockett is the sole character in *The Well of Loneliness* able to break through the tormented Stephen's seemingly inexhaustible reserves of hypocrisy, self-deception, and erotic *morbidezza*. Long before Stephen acknowledges her lesbianism to herself or anyone else, Brockett recognizes it for her and, amid camp and badinage, delicately steers her toward self-awareness. Early on, when they meet as fellow writers, he accuses her of letting a "horrid dry rot" infect her style and hints that her sexual self-denial is to blame (231). She needs "life," he tells her, and by exhorting her to move to Paris, where she will meet the lesbian *salonnière* Valérie Seymour and begin her first full-blown love affair—with the young ambulance driver Mary Llewellyn—he helps her to escape from a state of overwhelming psychic deadlock.

In the Paris scenes—though he flits in and out of view here as casually as Coward, an inveterate globetrotter, flitted in and out of

the lives of his many friends and associates—Brockett continues to
bring about epiphanies. In a novel obsessed with the "truth" of sexuality (how to speak it aloud, how to make it plain), he is the first
character who attempts to "say" homosexuality to Stephen in a way
that she can hear. He does so cautiously at first, when he takes her
(along with her old teacher Puddle) to visit Versailles soon after the
two women arrive in Paris (237–40). Guiding Stephen through the
apartments formerly belonging to Marie Antoinette, recreating in

45

Disconcertingly clever: a) Coward in a Brockett-like pose b) by Cecil Beaton, 1930s

her mind "the image of the luckless queen . . . as though for some reason this unhappy woman must appeal in a personal way to Stephen," he calls attention to some mantelpiece trinkets given to the queen by her devoted friend, the Princesse de Lamballe:

> 'Madame de Lamballe gave those to the queen,' he murmured.
> She nodded, only vaguely apprehending his meaning.
> Presently they followed him out into the gardens and stood looking across the Tapis Vert that stretches its quarter mile of greenness towards a straight, lovely line of water. Brockett said, very low, so that Puddle should not hear him: 'Those two would often come here at sunset. Sometimes they were rowed along the canal in the sunset—can't you imagine it, Stephen? They must often have felt pretty miserable, poor souls; sick to death of the subterfuge and pretences. Don't you ever get tired of that sort of thing? My God, I do!' But she did not answer, for now there was no mistaking his meaning. (239)

The passage is a fascinating one—and not only for what it tells us about early twentieth-century lesbian iconography. Rumors of Marie Antoinette's homosexuality circulated widely in England and France at the turn of the century: her passionate yet doomed friendships with the Princesse de Lamballe and the Comtesse de Polignac in the years leading up to the French Revolution had become the stuff of popular sentimental legend. Lesbian writers like Radclyffe Hall clearly regarded the French queen as an underground heroine—a tragic emblem of persecuted female-female desire.[45] Yet it is Brockett, rather than any explicitly lesbian character, who uses the figure of the queen to break through Stephen's emotional isolation. With a single deft allusion, seemingly casually proffered, he manages to communicate both the fact of his own homosexuality and his sympathetic understanding of Stephen's similarly "inverted" nature.

Hall's gambit here may be a direct tribute to Coward—almost a kind of novelistic ventriloquism. For Coward, too, had special interest in the queen and the rumors about her intimate life. Writes Cole Lesley, his biographer and lifelong friend, of Coward's reading habits:

> His favourites of E. Nesbit were re-read annually and there were certain other books to which he constantly returned, of which Stefan Zweig's *Marie Antoinette* was one, and he also bought any and every other book about her. His reactions to the Zweig never varied: when about half way through he would say, 'I suppose Marie Antoinette was one of the silliest women who ever lived,' and then expatiate on her silliness until he came to the flight to Varennes. From then on he became more and more moved by her increasing courage and sweetness of character in adversity, and finally by her unassailable dignity at her trial and execution.[46]

In the first part of his autobiography, *Present Indicative* (1937), Coward describes discovering a volume of "secret memoirs" relating to Marie Antoinette at a country house party in 1919 and reading them "luxuriously" while fellow guests went duck shooting.[47] The volume here seems to have been the pseudonymously authored *Secret Memoirs of Princess Lamballe* (1901), a largely fictional, highly sensationalized account of Marie Antoinette's passion for the ill-fated Lamballe. Like Zweig's later biography, *Secret Memoirs* made no bones about the homoerotic nature of the queen's friendships.[48] And by 1922 Coward himself was in print on the subject. In *A Withered Nosegay*, a book of mock historical portraits of ten supposedly notorious femme fatales (Donna Isabella Angelica Y Bananas, Maggie McWhistle, Anna Podd, Furstin Lieberwurst zu Schweinen-Kalber, and others), he devoted the first chapter to "Julie de Poopinac," a madcap composite of the Princesse de Lamballe and Comtesse de Polignac. Here is his account of Poopinac's arrival at Versailles and first encounter with Marie Antoinette—in which he parodies to perfection the *Secret Memoirs'* ludicrous mixture of breathlessness and pedantry:

What vice! What intrigue! What corruption! Versailles seemed but a vast conservatory sheltering the vile soil from which sprang the lilies of France—La Belle France, as Edgar Sheepmeadow so eloquently puts it. Did any single bloom escape the blight of ineffable depravity? No—not one! Occasionally some fresh young thing would appear at Court— appealing and innocent. Then the atmosphere would begin to take effect: some one would whisper something to her—she would leer almost unconsciously; a few days later she would be discovered carrying on anyhow!

Julie de Poopinac, beautiful, accomplished and incredibly witty, queened it in this mêlée of appalling degeneracy; she was not at heart wicked, but her environment closed in upon her pinched and wasted heart, crushing the youth and sweetness from it.

All the world knows of her celebrated scene with Marie Antoinette, but Edgar Sheepmeadow recounts it so deliciously in volume III of "Women Large and Women Small" that it would be a sin not to quote it. "They met," he says, "on the Grand Staircase. The Dauphine, with her usual hauteur, was mounting with her head held high. Julie, by some misfortune, happened to get in her way. The Dauphine, not seeing her, trod heavily on her foot, then jogged her in the ribs with her elbow. Though realising who it was, the great lady could not but apologise. Drawing herself up as high as possible, she said in icy tones, 'I beg your pardon!' Quick as thought Julie replied, 'Granted as soon as asked!' Then with a toss of her curls, she ran down the stairs, leaving the haughty Princess's mind a vortex of tumultuous feelings."[49]

The manner here, admittedly, is a bit different from Brockett's in *The Well of Loneliness*. While still recognizably Coward-like, Brockett is more the sentimental Antoinette devotee described by Cole Lesley. But one's sense of an identity tag is strong. Coward's absorption in the martyred queen—comic, tragic, idiosyncratic— translates into Brockett's carefully dramatized history lesson. The result is a scene—in Hall—of double demystification: in Brockett's tact and intelligence there is more than a hint of the playwright's gaiety and moral candor, in Stephen's alert and encompassing listening, a suggestion of Radclyffe Hall's emotional debt to the man who encouraged her by his own example to write more openly about homosexuality.

Brockett's truth telling plays an important part later in the novel too; after "teaching" Stephen Paris and introducing her to Valérie Seymour, he remains an eloquent and empathetic witness to the difficult, unfolding dramas of her erotic life, especially after she embarks on her doomed love affair with Mary Llewellyn, the young Welsh girl from her wartime ambulance unit. In the penultimate stages of the narrative in particular, one welcomes his reappearances precisely because he projects a voice of common sense—of sociability, lightness, and psychic resilience—in a world becoming steadily darker and more alienating. He is warm and graceful, for example, when he meets Mary unexpectedly, soon after the armistice, and realizes that she and Stephen are now living together at Stephen's house on the Rue Jacob:

> He did not stay embarrassingly late, nor did he leave suggestively early; he got up to go at just the right moment. But when Mary went out of the room to call Pierre, he quite suddenly put his arm through Stephen's.
>
> 'Good luck, my dear, you deserve it,' he murmured, and his sharp grey eyes had grown almost gentle: 'I hope you'll be very, very happy.' (330)

(Stephen, who disengages her arm here "with a look of surprise" and a stifled "Thank you, Brockett," is characteristically tight-lipped and gauche in response.) Later, when Stephen's relationship with Mary begins slowly, painfully, to deteriorate—Stephen cannot rid herself of the crippling burden of self-hatred and sexual guilt—Brockett

The Well's homosexual underworld: lesbian
patrons of Le Monocle, Boulevard Edgar-Quinet,
Montparnasse, by Brassaï, 1932

valiantly tries to save the day. Stephen has been throwing herself into her work, leaving Mary to her own sad devices. Brockett objects:

'You're not playing fair with that girl; the life she's leading would depress a mother abbess. It's enough to give anybody the hump, and it's going to give Mary neurasthenia!'

'What on earth do you mean?'

'Don't get ratty and I'll tell you. Look here, I'm not going to pretend any more. Of course we all know that you two are lovers. You're gradually becoming a kind of legend—all's well lost for love, and that sort of thing. . . . But Mary's too young to become a legend; and so are you, my dear, for that matter. But you've got your work, whereas Mary's got nothing—not a soul does that miserable kid know in Paris. Don't *please* interrupt, I've nearly finished; I positively

must and will have my say out! You and she have decided to make a ménage—as far as I can see it's as bad as marriage! But if you were a man it would be rather different; you'd have dozens of friends as a matter of course. Mary might even be going to have an infant. Oh, for God's sake, Stephen, do stop looking shocked. Mary's a perfectly normal young woman; she can't live by love alone—that's all rot—especially as I shrewdly suspect that when you're working the diet's pretty meagre. For heaven's sake let her go about a bit! Why on earth don't you take her to Valérie Seymour's? At Valérie's place, she'd meet lots of people; and I ask you, what harm could it possibly do?' (346)

The lack of hypocrisy here—Brockett's "of course we all know that you two are lovers" resounds across the rest of novel as one of its few really liberating utterances—both impels Stephen to action (she will try to save the love affair with Mary) and provokes one's readerly gratitude. Finally: someone to give this insufferable woman, with her inane "manly" reserve and self-crucifying attitudes, the goods—with bells on.

Of course it's not good enough. Indeed, one will object, Brockett's remains ultimately the most *un*heeded voice in the novel. He can do nothing in the end to allay Stephen's gloom, just as nothing can stop Hall's narrative from taking its own seemingly inevitable and piteous course. In the same way that Hall's homosexual characters bear the visible signs of their sexual "morbidity" (pale white hands, thick ankles, voices too high or too low), so the narrative itself seems marked: unbalanced and out of sync—"ill" in an almost endocrinal sense. Moments of joy are contaminated before they can even register on the psyche; the yearning for freedom results in pain and scarification, a corrugation of the heart.

In the end, Brockett simply has to opt out—out of his friend's life and out of the novel. He exits precisely at the start of its final cri-

Noël Coward &
Radclyffe Hall

sis: as Stephen, avid for despair and accompanied by their "invert" friends Dickie and Wanda, takes Mary on a deranged, infernal tour of the Parisian homosexual underworld. Brockett joins them, his eyes "coldly observant" yet troubled too, at a Stygian local boîte—Le Narcisse—where the walls are "hung with mirrors thickly painted with cupids, thickly sullied by flies," couples weave about drunkenly on a tiny dance floor, and "a faint blend of odours . . . wafted from the kitchen which stood in proximity to the toilet" (385). (And thus, if crudely, Hall anticipates the caliginous, neo-Baudelairean scenery of Djuna Barnes's *Nightwood*.)

Yet Brockett leaves almost as soon as he appears, disgusted by Stephen's self-inflicted misery. ("He was sulky, it seemed, because Stephen had snubbed him. He had not spoken for half an hour, and refused point blank to accompany them further. 'I'm going home to bed, thanks—good morning,' he said crossly, as they crowded into the motor" [387].) His departure signals the imminent turn of the novel toward melodrama, for Stephen, contorted with guilt, will not long after give Mary up—to a man—after a series of blatantly implausible plot twists. But Brockett's exit can also be read as allegory—as the sign of his delayed and self-protective realization that he is in the wrong novel, that he cannot flourish in such a fetid, claustrophobic fictional world, that he is ill suited to the obsessional adumbration of homosexual despair. Radclyffe Hall lets him go.

Or does she? If Brockett's role is to represent a world of non-melodramatic possibility—of humor, friends, love, work, sex, and the peace of mind that comes with the ultimately banal recognition that there may be someone after all to cherish one's human presence on the earth—he makes *The Well of Loneliness* something other, paradoxically, than what it is. However intermittently, he represents a salutary incoherence, a rebuff to the dire. One must stress the intermittency, of course: as a number critics have pointed out, Hall's portrait of Brockett remains a contradictory one. The numerous references to Brockett's emotional vampirism, his "feeding" on the psychic lives of other people, even the fetishistic, somewhat repellent descriptions of his "feminine"-looking hands, suggest an authorial ambivalence that is never satisfactorily resolved. Nor is Hall able to give Brockett a lover of his own; alone among the major homosexual characters in the book, he remains conspicuously without a sexual partner and as discreet about his own love life as he is curious about Stephen's. No "Mad About the Boy" for him.

Yet when one looks at what Brockett actually does—at the kind of psychological agency with which he is associated—one can't help finding him, along with Stephen's governess, Puddle, the book's most wholesome, valuable, even therapeutic presence. The otherwise favorably rendered Valérie Seymour is compromised by

Beresford Egan's caricature of Radclyffe
Hall after the publication of
The Well of Loneliness, 1928

The Beresford Egan cartoon lampooning *The Well of Loneliness* that so shocked John her involvement in Stephen's masochistic scheme to alienate Mary at the novel's bitter close; Brockett, on the contrary, functions purely benevolently. He is like a shaman figure in folk tale or myth, a helper character who magically aids and abets. *The Well* itself, it turns out, is against him: he inhabits a story in which "loneliness"— the inability to let oneself be consoled—has been determined in advance as the defining feature of homosexual experience. He belongs in some other work—*The Well of Sociability*, perhaps, or *The Well of Feeling Better*, or *The Well of Having a Good Time*.

Comedy was not entirely foreign to Radclyffe Hall; her third novel, *A Saturday Life*, published in 1925, is essentially a comic piece, written in the same whimsical period vein as Vita Sackville-West's *Seducers in Ecuador* (1924) or Sylvia Townsend Warner's *Lolly Willowes* (1926). If only for a moment, the antimelancholic figure of Brockett lets us imagine the novel Radclyffe Hall might have written—in 1928—had she been able to resist the sickly allure of polemic and incorporate into her fiction more of her own not-so-tragic lesbian life. Hall undoubtedly had a martyr complex— her outraged response to Beresford Egan's caricature of her as a lesbian Christ on the cross during the *Well* trial suggests he had hit home more than she liked to admit—but her life on the whole, even after the banning of her novel, was an equable one. She was the sort of woman—stylish, sensitive, artistically gifted, much esteemed by intelligent people—who had friends like Noël Coward. In her 1961 memoir of Hall, Una Troubridge reflected on the pleasures of their long emotional partnership: the trips taken, the meals eaten, the musical works enjoyed, and the art works admired, even the mock heroic triumphs of their numerous beloved show dogs. ("Thora was dead but we had Thorgils of Tredholt, another red dachshund bought by John at a Brighton dog show. He became a big winner and was presently joined by

Wotan who as Champion Fitz-John Wotan helped to make dachshund history.") And she was not afraid to memorialize moments of sheer comic rapture:

> On our way to Avignon there was another pleasant incident. The day was tropical and we were terribly hot and thirsty, beginning to wilt and to long for the next stop, when we drove through the village of Châteauneuf du Pape and right through the middle of their cherry market. Cherries were everywhere in gigantic baskets, hundreds and thousands of kilos of ripe cherries and we clamoured to Pierre to go at once and buy some. He came back with a crestfallen face to say that the sale was only *'en gros'* . . . but it took more than that to discourage us and when he had ascertained that the minimum sale was ten kilos we had them poured into the bottom of the car and ate them steadily all the way to Avignon, throwing the stones and stalks into the road . . . we sat with our feet submerged in cherries.[50]

Morbid? One can imagine Brockett's (and Coward's) "hoots" of companiable laughter.

> Nobody quite understands
> The strange irresolute glands
> Of a big girl—like me.
> —Noël Coward, "I Wish I Wasn't Quite Such a Big Girl," 1946[51]

Given his lifelong sapphophilia, it is not surprising that Coward's stories, poems, and plays are full of such "big girls," longing for sweet wives to console them:

> HENRIETTA: *If I were a man I would marry a wife*
> *Who would help me to lead an exemplary life*

And the house that I'd build
Would be pleasantly filled
With children belonging to me.
It would also command
Several acres of land
And an excellent view of the sea
A most excellent view of the sea.

GEORGINA: *If I were a man I'd go out in the dawn*
And I'd gaze at the curve of the bay
And I'd write in a book
How the mountains look
At the beginning of the day.
If I were a man
I should wish to be born
With a dream that would set me apart
And I'd search the world over
To find my true lover
And give her my passionate heart![52]

One thinks of poor Stephen Gordon—longing for manhood, domesticity, and a mate with whom to share love's glories: "All things they would be the one to the other, should they stand in that limitless relationship; father, mother, friend, and lover, all things—the amazing completeness of it; and Mary, the child, the friend, the beloved" (300).

But the representation of lesbianism in Coward's work is at once more multifaceted and more personal. Of course not every reference to love between women in his writing should be read as a coded allusion to Radclyffe Hall: sapphic motifs were there in his work from the beginning, even in early confections like *A Withered*

Nosegay (1922).* From one angle the prominence of the theme in Coward's writing was simply a reflection of the growing cultural visibility of female homosexuality in England in the postwar years. The First World War, with its moral and social upheavals, had liberated homosexual women; as Hall put it in *The Well*, lesbians had begun to creep from their "holes" into the "daylight" and form tentative new communities (271).[53]

Coward, it is true, lived in a cosmopolitan milieu where such transformations were particularly evident, but he was hardly alone in responding imaginatively to the new lesbian presence in British society. From James Huneker's *Painted Veils* (1920), Elizabeth Russell's *The Enchanted April* (1922), Ronald Firbank's *The Flower Beneath the Foot* (1923), Virginia Woolf's *Mrs. Dalloway* (1925), and Naomi Royde-Smith's *The Tortoise-Shell Cat* (1925) to Elizabeth Bowen's *The Hotel* (1927), Compton Mackenzie's *Extraordinary Women* (1928), Woolf's *Orlando* (1928), Wyndham Lewis's *The Apes of God* (1930), Molly Keane's *Devoted Ladies* (1934), and Sylvia Townsend Warner's *Summer Will Show* (1936), Anglo-American literature of the 1920s and 1930s is full of sapphic local color. (Indeed, *Extraordinary Women*, Mackenzie's brilliant but now forgotten spoof of expatriate lesbian society on Capri, is nothing *but* sapphic local color.) Even before *The Well's* publication, overtly lesbian characters, like the androgynous Geraldine Manners in Rosamond Lehmann's *Dusty Answer* (1927)— short-haired, "masculine" in appearance, yet with a strange seductive power over susceptible female companions—had become a staple in both the serious and popular fiction of the day.[54]

Noël Coward &
Radclyffe Hall

*Perhaps the influence here ran the other way: Coward's comical predilection for soggy mock poetical locutions such as "the well of truth" may have had something to do, if only subliminally, with Hall's magnificently kitschy title. "My heart is a pool of ecstasy," one of Coward's mock heroines, Sarah, Lady Tunnell-Penge, exclaims, and Coward, in the guise of sentimental biographer, follows with a typical comic apostrophe, "Pitiful pool, so soon to be drained of its joy!" See *A Withered Nosegay*, pp. 8 and 49. In *Virginia Woolf and the Languages of Patriarchy* Jane Marcus has offered the interesting theory that Hall's title is an ironic play on the Cave of Harmony, the famous Soho nightclub founded in 1917 by Elsa Lanchester and others. It may be that both Coward's and Hall's metaphoric locutions owe something to the Cave.

And yet the more one examines the careers of Hall and Coward in tandem, the more one gets the sense that it was Hall—the most famous and intransigently "sapphic" personality of the postwar years—who most deeply influenced Coward's sometimes arch, sometimes plangent representations of lesbian experience. If Coward's references to contemporary lesbian life occasionally appear generic—and it is true, an awful lot of women with Eton crops and tailored suits pop up in his fiction and plays—we need to remember how central a role Hall the public figure played in creating the classic image of the 1920s lesbian. Other women might cut

Hall in profile by Howard Coster, 1932

their hair or wear ties—the painter Gluck did, Sylvia Townsend Warner's lover Valentine Ackland did—but it was Hall who became notorious for it, whose picture appeared in popular weeklies, whose personal style became preeminently identified with "lesbian" style. *The Well of Loneliness* simply confirmed Hall's mascot status. In presenting her heroine's struggle for recognition in a series of stark, allegorical, easily assimilated, almost Bunyanesque episodes (Parental Disapproval, First Unhappy Love, Escape to the City, Discovery of Others Like Oneself, Second Unhappy Love, and so on), Hall established the standard tropes—moral and descriptive—on which other writers would draw obsessively for the next fifty years.

Coward's portraits of his friend and her circle are on the whole comic, even flippant at times: Coward typically makes gorgeous fun of Hall, as he does with all his characters, male and female, young and old, sophisticated and naive, homosexual and heterosexual. He is in

some ways a 1920s Theophrastus or Molière, captivated by comic types: the Female Ingenue, the Debonair Young Man (often of indeterminate sexual preference), the glamorous and embittered Heterosexual Woman in her Thirties (typically played, of course, by Gertrude Lawrence), the Addled Husband (Elyot in *Private Lives* or Charles in *Blithe Spirit*). The Butch Lady Writer might be considered simply one in his arsenal of contemporary Theophrastian types. But at the same time, even when she is merely a backdrop character, Coward's Hall-influenced portraits often carry a particular emotional charge—a peculiar affectionate identification or sense of things unsaid. And in at least one instance—as I will argue in relation to *Blithe Spirit*—she plays a crucial, even Muselike role, if only behind the scenes, in the private workshop of Coward's imagination. There Radclyffe Hall, visionary defender of same-sex love, is indeed a ghost in the machine—the spiritual adviser, as it were, to Coward the gay moralist and subversive commentator on modern sexual relations.

Coward's first important evocation of Hall and her circle appears in the unproduced 1926 play *Semi-Monde*, written two years into their friendship. Though Hall cannot be identified outright with any specific character, Coward gestures toward her and the glamorous international lesbian milieu in which she moved. Set in the Ritz Hotel in Paris over a period of a year and a half, *Semi-Monde* turns upon the romantic groupings and regroupings of a number of couples, including both male and female homosexuals. The context is briskly satirical: Coward observes the five lesbian characters in the play—the opera singer Inez Zulieta, Inez's unfaithful lover Cynthia Gable, Cynthia's young inamorata Elise Trent, their flirtatious friend Marion Fawcett, and Violet Emery, whom

Lesbian and gay high life between the wars: *Private View* by Gladys Hines, showing Hall and Troubridge in center, 1937

Inez seduces after separating from Cynthia—with his usual sardonic eye. The erotic chopping and changing between the five is comical and continuous, with the petulant, vermouth-addicted Inez—who sheds and attaches lovers with operatic abandon—at the center of the emotional turmoil. And all five speak in high Cowardese: when Marion asks Inez and Cynthia if they have seen "a dark little American girl with a sort of wood violet face loitering about," Inez—who hates her—replies acidly, "Yes, hundreds."[55]

The bitchy travails of Inez and her crowd bring to mind Hall's own description of the lesbian cocktail set in the Paris sections of *The Well*:

> And now [Brockett] was launched on a torrent of gossip about people of whom Stephen had never even heard: 'Pat's been deserted—have you heard that, darling? Do you think she'll take the veil or cocaine or something? One never quite knows what may happen next with such an emotional temperament, does one? Arabella's skipped off to the Lido with Jane Grigg. The Grigg's just come into pots and pots of money, so I hope they'll be delirious and silly while it lasts—I mean the money. . . . Oh, and have you heard about Rachel Morris? They say . . . ' He flowed on and on like a brook in spring flood. (245)

But Coward's rendering of sapphic high life may be rather more pointed than Hall's own. Hall was devoted to opera and singing: her former lover Mabel Batten had been a semiprofessional singer, and Hall was friendly throughout her life with a number of lesbian opera stars. (Natalie Barney, the model for Valérie Seymour in *The Well*, was an important go-between; among the regular guests at Barney's all-female Paris salon before and after the First World War was the celebrated French diva Emma Calvé.[56])

At the very least the fact that the opera-singing Inez uses her histrionic gift to attract new lovers—witness the capture of the starstruck Violet in act 3—suggests a tie-in with the larger lesbian "gossip world" that Hall and Una Troubridge inhabited in the 1920s and 1930s. At the same time—perhaps more subtly—Coward may also be hinting at Hall's own romantic entanglements, such as the troubled liaison with Batten, whom Hall had abandoned (as he would have known) for Troubridge in 1915.[57]

The opera-singing Mabel Batten ("Ladye")
painted by John Singer Sargent, 1895

Four "poets" from *Spangled Unicorn*,
clockwise: a) E. A. I. Maunders b) Crispin Pither
c) Jane Southerby Danks d) Juana Mandragagita

Hall materializes more fully in Coward's parody anthology of modernist verse, *Spangled Unicorn* (1932). Billed as "a selection from the works of Albrecht Drausler, Serge Lliavanov, Janet Urdler, Elihu Dunn, Ada Johnston, Jane Southerby Danks, Tao Lang Pee, E. A. I. Maunders, Crispin Pither, and Juana Mandragagita," *Spangled Unicorn* is a collection of mostly nonsensical parodies of T. S. Eliot, Ezra Pound, Edith Sitwell, Gertrude Stein, and others. Each group of poems is prefaced by a quasi-scholarly "biographical note" and a photograph of the author in question. The parodies are often witty, but the authors' pictures remain the most amusing feature of the volume: Coward bought a batch of outlandish old photos of unknown people from a London junk shop and simply matched one to each poet. After the book was published, he had to pay damages to various individuals who claimed to recognize deceased loved ones in the images.[58]

Here we do find a recognizable portrait of Hall: in the section of the book devoted to the farouche, to-hounds-riding "poetess" Jane Southerby Danks. "Danks" suggests the supersaturated world of *The Well*, while the name in full hints at "Marguerite Radclyffe Hall," under which she published five books of poetry—*'Twixt Earth and Stars*, *A Sheaf of Verses*, *Poems of the Past and Present*, *Songs of Three Counties and Other Poems*, and *The Forgotten Island*— between 1906 and 1915. (Hall dispensed with the "Marguerite" when she began publishing novels in 1924.) Coward confirms the link in his mock biographical preface to Southerby Danks's poems:

> Born in Melton Mowbray in 1897 she rode to hounds constantly, wet or fine, from the age of four onwards. Blauie's portrait "Musette on Roan" depicts her at the very beginning of her adolescence. From the first she shunned the company of the male sex, mixing only with her governesses. To one of whom Madeleine Duphotte she dedicated her first volume of Poems, *Goose Grass*. The Dedication is illuminating in its profound simplicity—"To you, Madeleine, from me."[59]

The send-up is blatant—both of *The Well of Loneliness* and of Hall's own life. Danks's equestrianism links her at once with the youthful Stephen Gordon, who from an early age rides to hounds "with a fire in her heart that made life a thing of glory" (60); Hall herself nearly broke her neck while hunting in 1908. "Madeleine Duphotte" recalls Mademoiselle Duphot, the little French governess whom Stephen loves yet bewilders with her incessant tomboyish chatter on "splints and spavins, cow hocks and colics" and other equine ailments (55). And like both Stephen and her creator, the eccentric Southerby Danks is a wanderer—forced from home by a rejecting mother and condemned to a life of exile in strange places:

> Storm clouds in her relations with her mother began to gather on the horizon as early as 1912, indeed in the May of this year we find her in Florence with Hedda Jennings then at the height of her career. Her emancipation from home ties continued and the breach had obviously broadened in 1916 when we find her writing from a whaler off Helsinforth to Mrs. Hinton Turner (Libelulle) at Saint Cloud. "How I envy you in your green quiet room. Here, no lace no Sheffield plate, only tar and the cry of gulls, but my heart is easier." 1924 finds her cosily ensconced in Boulogne where she first gained from the fisher-folk the appellation "Knickerbocker Lady." In 1925 she published *Hands Down* to be followed in the Spring of 1926 by *Frustration*.[60]

Opera appears again—in the mention of Hedda Jennings "at the height of her career"—as is Mabel Batten, whose married name, Mrs. George Batten, and nickname, Ladye, may both be echoed in "Mrs. Hinton Turner (Libelulle)." The knickerbockers recall Hall's predilection for fashionable menswear, while *Hands Down* and *Frustration* could almost be comic retitlings of *The Well* itself.

Danks's author photograph, interestingly enough, features the most androgynous-looking individual in *Spangled Unicorn*—a smirking personage in pearls, dressed in a bizarre Turkish costume reminiscent of the outfits worn by the sex-changing heroine of Woolf's *Orlando* (1928). It is difficult to tell if the sitter is male or female; he/she gazes at the viewer ambiguously, with a coy come-hitherism altogether lacking in the portraits, say, of "Crispin Pither" or "Juana Mandragagita." Since Coward seems to have selected his author photos on the grounds of general silliness—to layer absurdity upon absurdity—he may have chosen this ludicrously incongruous image simply because it is the *least* like the rather earnest personage described in the Danks biographical note. But in assigning this androgynous form to Danks, perhaps he was also responding at some level to Hall's own ambiguous sexual persona.

Alas, of the four poems in *Spangled Unicorn* ascribed to Jane Southerby Danks, none bears much resemblance to any real Radclyffe Hall poem. Like her contemporary Vita Sackville-West, whose conservative political and artistic leanings she shared, Hall wrote poems traditional in form and feeling.[61] Coward makes no effort to mimic her actual poetic style. The literary satire in *Spangled Unicorn* is directed at more flamboyant experimental writers: Gertrude Stein—who appears as "E. A. I. Maunders"—and Edith Sitwell, whose whimsical-surreal mode can be recognized in the nonsensical concoctions of "Janet Urdler" and "Ada Johnson." Danks, too, often sounds Sitwellian—as in the exquisitely moronic "Legend":

Slap the cat and count the spinach
Aunt Matilda's gone to Greenwich
Rolling in a barrel blue
Harnessed to a Kangaroo
Pock-marked Ulysses approaches
Driving scores of paper coaches
Eiderdowns and soda-water
What a shame that Mrs. Porter
Lost her ticket for the play
(Aunt Matilda's come to stay)

Prod the melons, punch the grapes
See that nobody escapes.[62]

Nonetheless, there are occasional traces of the poetical Hall to be found. In the ridiculous "Old Things Are Far the Best," Danks's ludicrous elaboration of sentimental feeling—"Though Grandmamma may dribble / Don't point at her and laugh / She gave you Auntie Sybil / A train and a giraffe—/ Old things are far the best"— might remind a less than pious reader of the emotional and stylistic bathos so often afflicting both Hall's poetry and prose.[63]

From Coward's other writings of the '20s and '30s it is possible to compile an anthology of Radclyffe Hall moments—comic flash points when he seems to be responding either to her directly or to the burgeoning culture of "extraordinary women" represented so vividly and forthrightly in her fiction. Hall and her circle may have been in Coward's mind, for example, when he wrote the gender-bending lyrics for the song "Britannia Rules the Waves," performed by Maisie Gay in the 1928 revue *This Year of Grace*:

The British male
May often fail,
Our faith in sport is shaken,
So English girls awaken
And save the nation's bacon.

Up girls and at 'em
And play the game to win,
The men must all give in
Before the feminine.
Bowl 'em and bat 'em
And put them on the run,
Defeat them every one,
Old Caspar's work is done.
We'll do our bit till our muscles crack,

We'll put a frill on the Union Jack,
If Russia has planned
To conquer us and America misbehaves,
Up girls and at 'em,
Britannia rules the waves!

Coward's giddy paean to virile British females "saving the nation's bacon" puts one in mind of Hall's friend, Barbara ("Toupie") Lowther, the dashing lesbian daughter of the Earl of Lonsdale. Lowther ran a women's volunteer ambulance corps on the western front in the First World War and was later decorated for her services with the Croix de Guerre. Hall drew on her friend's exploits in the 1926 short story "Miss Ogilvy Finds Herself," and in

Toupie Lowther's WWI female ambulance corps

the World War I scenes of *The Well* modeled the all-female Break-speare Ambulance Unit, in which Stephen proudly serves with her young lover Mary, on Lowther's mostly lesbian brigade:

> They might look a bit odd, indeed some of them did, and yet in the streets they were seldom stared at, though they strode a little, perhaps from shyness, or perhaps from a slightly self-conscious desire to show off, which is often the same thing as shyness. They were part of the universal convulsion and were being accepted as such, on their merits. And although their Sam Browne belts remained swordless, their hats and their caps without regimental badges, a battalion was formed in those terrible years that would never again be completely disbanded. War and death had given them a right to life, and life tasted sweet, very sweet to their palates. Later on would come bitterness, disillusion, but never again would such women submit to being driven back to their holes and corners. (271–72)

Coward, characteristically, takes a rather more facile approach— "Here's to the maid / Who isn't afraid, / Who shingles and shoots and shaves. / Up girls and at 'em, / Britannia rules the waves!"[64]— but in the exuberance of the sentiment pays a backhanded compliment to the androgynous "new women" liberated by war. In assigning the lyric to a woman ("Maisie Gay triumphed," he wrote in his memoirs, "with her channel-swimmer song 'Up Girls and At 'Em'"), he also hints at the new kinds of loving—heroically homosexual—with which such martial aplomb could be linked.

In the well-known cabaret song "I've Been to a Marvellous Party"—from the revised version of *Words and Music* staged in New York in 1938 and originally written for Beatrice Lillie—Coward draws once again on the jaded homosexual high life scenes in the Paris section of *The Well*:

> *I've been to a marvellous party*
> *With Nounou and Nada and Nell,*

It was in the fresh air
And we went as we were
Which was Hell.
Poor Grace started singing at midnight
And didn't stop singing till four;
We knew the excitement was bound to begin
When Laura got blind on Dubonnet and gin
And scratched her veneer with a Cartier pin,
I couldn't have liked it more.

I've been to a marvellous party,
Elise made an entrance with May,
You'd never have guessed
From her fisherman's vest
That her bust had been whittled away.
Poor Lulu got fried on Chianti
And talked about esprit de corps.
Maurice made a couple of passes at Gus
And Freddie, who hates any kind of a fuss,
Did half the Big Apple and twisted his truss,
I couldn't have liked it more.[65]

And he returns to the same milieu in his mordant 1939 short story "What Mad Pursuit?" Coward's protagonist is a famous English writer, Evan Lorrimer, on a publicity tour of New York. As he's shepherded from party to party—each more alcohol soaked than the last—Stephen, Brockett, Valérie Seymour, Wanda, Mary, and the rest of *The Well*'s "army of inverts" seem to live again in Evan's checkered nocturnal progress through Manhattan's homosexual bohemia. There is Léonie, who has a Stephen-like "Eton crop" and is full of "jolly schoolboyish vitality"; Léonie's lover Shirley, strikingly handsome, à la Valérie Seymour, in "a perfectly plain gray flannel coat and skirt"; the effeminate designer George Tremlett, "a very pale young man in green Chinese pajamas"; the opera singer Irene Marlow, who regales the group with stories of her youthful crush on Geraldine Farrar; and an exotic French-woman, Suzanne Closanges, who writes "poetry either in French or English, she doesn't care which" and lives with another woman at a lavish house in the country, to which the bewildered Evan finds himself dragged as the dawn approaches. Coward's characters are as embroiled in drunken melodrama as any of their *Well* counter-parts. When Suzanne and Shirley proceed to have a jealous row (Suzanne is Léonie's former lover), they knock to the floor "a pho-tograph of a lady in a fencing costume." Even this may be a *Well*-related joke: Stephen Gordon is a "marvellous, champion fencer," whose skills regularly astound everyone from Mademoiselle Duphot to Valérie Seymour. As always, Coward's tone is lighter than Hall's—more acid and disengaged—but his scenes of excess and dismay are as compelling in their way as Hall's *tableau des moeurs modernes*.

Of course one could object that while undeniably reminiscent of Hall's fiction, such sapphic moments, including the explicit comic portrait of Hall in *Spangled Unicorn*, remain somewhat miscella-neous and impersonal. In "What Mad Pursuit?" Coward seems to make a brief, subterranean, quasi-autobiographical feint at her: Evan Lorrimer is in many ways a self-portrait—one of the least dis-guised in all his writing—and in Lorrimer's bemused odyssey through the New York branch of transatlantic lesbian and gay cul-ture, Coward offers a simulacrum of that cosmopolitan society he and Hall frequented in the raucous early '20s. Yet to call this oblique cross-reference to a shared world a "tribute" to Hall—in the sense that I have spoken of the Brockett portrait in *The Well* as an extended if ambivalent homage—may seem too histrionic. What we need is something beyond the odd Brassaï-like set piece of Cinzano-sipping ladies in gentlemen's clothing—something comparable to the complex, bittersweet depiction of Coward in Hall's novel. To find such an evocation we must turn to a later Coward work—one written, as it turned out, only two years before Hall's death.

The celebrated 1941 farce, *Blithe Spirit*, in which an urbane novelist, Charles Condomine, accidentally conjures up the ghost of his dead wife at a seance, then is driven to distraction when she and his living wife begin to bicker over him, remains Coward's best-known piece of theatrical writing and the work upon which, more than any other, his reputation as a comic dramatist continues to rest. Like *The Well*, *Blithe Spirit* has taken on an almost metonymic relationship to its creator—its very title summing up popular perceptions of the effervescent Coward persona. Yet this, paradoxically, the most Coward-like of all Coward's works, is also permeated most thoroughly by the spirit of Radclyffe Hall. Not that the association will seem immediately transparent: one will look in vain through the dramatis personae of *Blithe Spirit* for any roman à clef portrait of the lesbian novelist. Yet she haunts it no less palpably than Noël Coward haunts *The Well* in the form of Jonathan Brockett.

The crucial evidence I will put forward in support of this claim is ghostly indeed: that uncanny document mentioned briefly in the first part of this essay—the 215-page report "On a Series of Sittings with Mrs. Osborne Leonard," published by Hall and Troubridge in the *Proceedings of the Society for Psychical Research* (SPR) in December 1919. Hall and Troubridge, we recall, had become lovers in 1915, while Hall was still involved with the fifty-eight-year-old Batten. With Batten's sudden death the following year, the guilty pair sought out a professional London medium, Mrs. Osborne Leonard of Maida Vale, in the hope of contacting Batten and making amends. Mrs. Leonard came recommended by Sir Oliver Lodge, vice president of the Society for Psychical Research, who in his best-selling book, *Raymond: or Life and Death* (1916), had

Lover and seance-partner:
a) Una Troubridge in
1914; and b) with bust of
Nijinsky

a) Mrs. Gladys Osborne Leonard, Hall and Troubridge's personal medium b) Leonard with Sir Oliver Lodge, vice president of the Society for Psychical Research, around 1920

described how Leonard had succeeded in contacting his son, an officer killed in World War I.[66] Almost immediately Batten began "speaking" with Hall and Troubridge—sometimes through "the table" (by rapping in response to questions) and sometimes by way of Mrs. Leonard's "spirit control," "Feda," a young Indian girl who had supposedly died around 1800.[67] Convinced of the authenticity of the messages received—Mrs. Leonard in her trance states seemed to know things about them that Hall and Troubridge were positive she could not have learned in advance—they began attending seances with her two or three times a week. One of them took notes at each sitting, and during the next three years they compiled a mass of material relating to the sessions. With Lodge's encouragement, they presented a preliminary report on their "findings" at two SPR meetings in 1917, then drew up a longer and far more detailed version for the society's journal in 1919.[68]

The published account was still a heavily censored one: in order to conceal the fact that the links between the three women were sexual, Hall and Troubridge left the nature of some of Batten's supposed communications unspecified, on the ground that they were "too personal." (They also referred to her throughout as "A.V.B." rather than "M.V.B."—her real initials—in order to make her identity less obvious.) But even in this compromised form, the SPR report remains a fascinating document—witness to Hall and Troubridge's often fantastic gullibility (the redoubtable Mrs. Leonard seems in fact to have been nothing more than a very canny, high-class charlatan) and to the workings of Hall's novelistic imagination.[69] Readers of Hall's fiction, for example, will notice at once how often significant events mentioned in the report reappear in altered form in her novels: during one sitting in 1916, for instance, Batten refers through Feda to a falling tree that killed a man outside a cottage she and Hall shared at Malvern Wells; Stephen's father, Sir Philip, is killed by a falling tree at the end of book 1 of *The Well*. Similarly, when Batten reminisces about a trip she and Hall took to Orotava on the island of Tenerife, we recognize the real-life model for the honeymoon trip Stephen and Mary Llewellyn make to Orotava in book 4.

That Coward was deeply interested in Hall and Troubridge's spiritualist exploits—to the point of taking their sessions with Mrs. Leonard as part of his immediate dramatic inspiration—seems to me most likely. There is evidence within *Blithe Spirit* itself to suggest that he was familiar with the SPR report and mined it for comic material. But at a more profound level the occult triangle between Hall, Batten, and Troubridge also informs what might be called the deep structure of his play. In the play, the novelist, Charles, in the company of his second wife, Ruth, and two friends, accidentally calls up the ghost of his first wife, Elvira, at an after-dinner seance conducted by a daffy local medium, Madame Arcati. Charles alone can see Elvira, and the comic confusions that ensue—Ruth becomes madly jealous of her invisible rival, who in turn wants to win Charles back by getting him over on the "Other Side"—are conditioned by the absurd interplay between the living and the dead.

The triangle here—a husband, in the company of his second wife, calls up the spirit of his first wife—resembles the Hall-Troubridge-Batten triangle in a displaced form. If we identify Hall with Charles, Batten with Elvira, Troubridge with Ruth, and Madame Arcati with Mrs. Leonard, the linkage becomes obvious: a "husband" (Hall/Charles), together with "his" second wife (Troubridge/Ruth), communicates via a medium (Madame Arcati/Mrs. Leonard) with "his" first wife (Batten/Elvira). In order to make the play acceptable for public consumption, Coward heterosexualizes it, but the romantic trio-plus-medium arrangement is the same.

The haunting of *Blithe Spirit* by the Hall-Troubridge-Batten configuration suggests at the outset that Coward's play is a rather more "lesbian" concoction than it is usually taken to be. It allegorizes Hall's uncanny relation with the two women who loved her in life and death. But it also allegorizes Hall's relation with Coward—in the shifting dynamic between Charles and the sublimely comic Madame Arcati. Indeed, through a series of fluid, mercurial, almost ectoplasmic identifications (Arcati is sometimes associated with Coward, at other times with Hall herself), Hall functions as a Lesbian Muse, who prompts Coward to some of his most penetrating and explicitly "gay" comic flights.

Before turning to these symbolic ramifications, however, let me suggest some ways in which Hall's spiritualist activities, obsessively documented and widely publicized in the SPR report, may have influenced Coward's basic comic schema. He was hardly the first British writer after the First World War to take up the spiritualist theme, of course, nor was *Blithe Spirit* the only work in which he addressed the issue. Since the mid-nineteenth century, spiritualism had attracted a huge popular following and dozens of distinguished literary adherents: Elizabeth Barrett Browning (who made her husband, Robert, accompany her to a seance led by the renowned medium D. D. Home in 1855), William James, J. W. Dunne, William Butler Yeats, and Arthur Conan Doyle. Even Coward's mother, Violet, was a believer: according to an entertaining anecdote related by Cole Lesley, not long after Coward began his acting career at the age of eleven, his mother attended a large public seance at the London Coliseum conducted by the thought reader Anna Eva Fay, whose speciality was taking questions from her audience while in a state of hypnotic trance. Feeling guilty about pushing her son onto the stage at the expense of his education, Mrs. Coward wrote out the question "Do you advise me to keep my son Noël Coward on the stage?" on a slip of paper and handed it to an usher at the start of the evening's performance. "There was a hush," writes Lesley, when Miss Fay at last appeared, draped in a sheet and with her arms "out wide" like a ghost:

> After answering one or two questions she shouted, 'Mrs. Coward! Mrs. Coward! You ask me about your son—keep him where he is! Keep him where he is! He has great talent and will have a wonder-

The passion for the occult: a seance scene from 1928

ful career!' After a few more questions, Miss Fay was near collapse and had to be helped off the stage. (18)

Not surprisingly, this bizarre experience instilled in Mrs. Coward—who remained flabbergasted for years afterward that Fay had selected her question out of the hundreds submitted—an undying belief that her son's stage career was meant to be.[70]

At the same time, however, spiritualism and its devotees inspired a seemingly inexhaustible body of satire—from Robert Browning's 1864 poem "Mr. Sludge, 'The Medium'" to T. S. Eliot's *The Waste Land* (1922), in which "Madame Sosostris," modeled in part on Madame Blavatsky, the notorious fake medium of the 1870s and 1880s, makes a hallucinatory (and discreditable) appearance. In *Queen Lucia* (1920), the first in his "Mapp and Lucia" series of comic novels, Radclyffe Hall's own Rye next door neighbor, E. F. Benson, satirized the spiritualist craze in the form of the Princess Popoffski, a Blavatsky-like medium whose "spirit control" is a little boy named Pocky who claims to have been a Hungarian violinist in a former life. Coward himself made fun of the spiritualist fad in the early two-

Madame Blavatsky (1831–1891), founder of the Theosophical Society and model for "Princess Popoffsky" and other comic mediums of the 1920s scene comic sketch *Weatherwise* (1923), via the unfortunate Lady Warple, who falls into a trance during a seance and upon awaking involuntarily barks like a dog whenever anyone mentions the weather. In *Still Life* (1936), the "refained" barmaid Myrtle Bagot is a devout believer in fortune tellers; and in *Present Laughter* (1939), the dotty housekeeper Miss Erikson has a female friend in Hammersmith with whom she conducts amateur seances—"they turn out all the lights, play the gramophone, and talk to an Indian."[71]

Without question, a lot of the spiritualist hocus-pocus Coward satirizes so broadly in *Blithe Spirit* might be considered generic: Madame Arcati's exotic "Eastern" monicker, the table-rapping code she uses to communicate with spirits ("one rap for yes—two raps for no"), the numerous references to materializations, spirit controls, "Elementals," and "the Other Side." Coward makes a comic point of his ease with the standard lingo in the following exchange from act 1 between Elvira, who has just abruptly materialized, and Charles, who is upset over the threat she poses to his marriage:

> CHARLES: Try to see my point, dear—I've been married to Ruth for five years, and you've been dead for seven . . .
>
> ELVIRA: Not dead, Charles—"passed over." It's considered vulgar to say "dead" where I come from.
>
> CHARLES: Passed over, then.[72]

But a number of details point to a deeper familiarity with the details of the Leonard sittings. True, Coward has updated things: *Blithe Spirit* is set in the present—not during the First World War years, when Hall and Troubridge began to see Mrs. Leonard. But he carefully changes the scene of the action to keep it consistent with Hall and Troubridge's (and Leonard's) whereabouts in the late 1930s. The play takes place in the Romney Marsh region in Kent—

The Forecastle, Radclyffe Hall's house in Rye in the 1930s

the Condomines live near Hythe; Hall and Troubridge lived in Rye,
a few miles down the coast. Madame Arcati, like Mrs. Leonard, has
been a "professional in London for years" but has recently moved
into the neighborhood; Mrs. Leonard, like Madame Arcati, moved
from Maida Vale to Tankerton, near Canterbury, in the early 1930s.
(After Leonard's relocation, Hall and Troubridge drove to see her
once a week, using a chauffeured car hired at the Rye garage.[73])

Describing Madame Arcati's delightfully inept "spirit control"
Daphne, whose protoplasmic bunglings in the other world are in
part responsible for Elvira's unexpected reappearance, Coward
seems to draw on Hall and Troubridge's colorful descriptions of
Mrs. Leonard's Feda. Both Feda and Daphne are mischievous

seven-year-olds, prone to jokes and tricks and zany little word games. Befitting her age and Indian background, Feda speaks "broken English," misspells certain words, and has her own "childish" way of putting things.[74] She refers to precious stones as "sparklies" and often exclaims over her love of bright colors and objects. ("This kind of elaboration," Hall and Troubridge observe in the SPR report, "nearly always seems to partake of the Oriental's childish love of gaudiness" [495–96]). Daphne, in turn, likes the baby rhyme "Little Tommy Tucker" and has to have it recited in singsong before she will answer any questions (28). The two share similar musical tastes: Feda is enraptured when she hears Batten singing popular songs in the spirit world (439); Daphne, Madame Arcati notes, is "more attached to Irving Berlin than anybody else—she likes a tune she can hum" (29). Daphne, it is true, is English rather than Indian, but one senses that Feda and her idiosyncrasies are not far from Coward's mind:

RUTH: Do you always have a child as a control?

MADAME ARCATI: Yes, they're generally the best—some mediums prefer Indians, of course, but personally I've always found them unreliable.

RUTH: In what way unreliable?

MADAME ARCATI: Well, for one thing they're frightfully lazy and also, when faced with any sort of difficulty, they're rather apt to go off into their own tribal language which is naturally unintelligible—that generally spoils everything and wastes a great deal of time. No, children are undoubtedly the more satisfactory, particularly when they get to know you and understand your ways. Daphne has worked for me for years. (24)

Similarly, Hall and Troubridge regard Feda's occasional pranks with tolerant amusement and write, "A very real mutual liking has grown up between ourselves and Feda. This, we have been given to understand, is not invariably the case" (346–47).

In staging the Condomine seance, Coward again may borrow certain details from the SPR account. Hall and Troubridge describe the entranced Mrs. Leonard falling from her chair at the start of a sitting as though "pitched" out of it by some unseen force (421); at the beginning of the Condomine seance, Madame Arcati gives

Scene from the first
London production of
Blithe Spirit (1941), with
Margaret Rutherford,
Kay Hammond,
and Fay Compton

a loud scream and falls unconscious to the floor (33). Awakening from her trance, Mrs. Leonard complains of cold and requires "a very large fire in the grate" (346); Madame Arcati "shivers" repeatedly and has to be plied with brandy in front of the fire (35). Most amusingly, Arcati, like her prototype, is oblivious to things that happen during the trance state: though the Condomines' dinner table falls to the floor "with a crash," objects fly around the room, and the ghostly Elvira makes herself known by saying "Good evening" to the terrified Charles in a "perfectly strange and charming voice," Madame Arcati will chirpily enquire at the end of it, "Well, what happened—was it satisfactory?" (35). Even Arcati's jolly postseance regimen of Ovaltine ("all ready in a saucepan at home—it only needs hotting up") may hark back to the Leonard sittings; Hall's biographer Michael Baker notes that Troubridge always made Ovaltine for "John" after a particularly strenuous session with Mrs. Leonard.[75]

Here and elsewhere, Coward's comic dialogues seem to echo the weird three-way conversations reproduced at numerous points in the spr report. Once Elvira appears (Charles can see and hear her, but Ruth can't), their bizarre triangular exchanges follow the pattern of those between Hall, Troubridge, and the deceased Batten. Although Leonard-as-Feda had the ability to mimic Batten's facial expressions and voice directly, her usual modus operandi was to act as a kind of "translator" for Batten, who remained invisible and inaudible.[76] Witness the following reported dialogue from a sitting in 1916 at which Batten informs Troubridge "through" Feda that she has just met Troubridge's dog Billy, recently put down and a new arrival in the spirit world:

F. She says, she's seen Billy and kissed him.

U.V.T. I'm glad.

F. She says Billy rubbed against her face. She says he didn't lick her face, she says that wouldn't have been very nice. She says he rubbed her with his muzzle. What does she mean by muzzle?

U.V.T. Well, ask her why she doesn't show you Billy?

F. Yes, Feda would like to see him. She says he's not very pretty. Is his mouth dark inside? (Here Feda indicates lips and gums.)

"John" and Una at the Ladies Kennel Club dog show at Ranelagh, 1920

u.v.t. Dark?

f. Yes, like liver colour, not pink colour, a kind of mottly colour, she thinks you ought to know.

u.v.t. Well, I'm not sure.

f. She says it was mottly inside, and she says, can't you ask someone who knows?

u.v.t. I will see. (490)

Coward seems to recreate the odd dynamic of the foregoing—Batten is "present" but can only "speak" through a third party—when he has Charles in act 2 pretend to "translate" what Elvira is saying for the increasingly jealous Ruth:

RUTH [*exasperated*] Where is Elvira at the moment?

CHARLES: In the chair, by the table.

RUTH: Now look here, Elvira—I shall have to call you Elvira, shan't I? I can't very well go on saying Mrs. Condomine all the time, it would sound too silly—

ELVIRA: I don't see why not.

RUTH: Did she say anything?

CHARLES: She said she'd like nothing better.

ELVIRA [*giggling*]: You really are sweet Charles darling—I worship you.

RUTH: I wish to be absolutely honest with you, Elvira—

ELVIRA: Hold on to your hats, boys!

RUTH: I admit I did ask Madame Arcati here with a view to getting you exorcized and I think that if you were in my position you'd have done exactly the same thing—wouldn't you?

ELVIRA: I shouldn't have done it so obviously.

RUTH: What did she say?

CHARLES: Nothing—she just nodded and smiled.

RUTH [*with a forced smile*]: Thank you, Elvira—that's generous of you. I really would so much rather that there were no misunderstandings between us—

CHARLES: That's very sensible, Ruth—I agree entirely. (68)

Coward tips the triangular situation here over into outright farce, yet the SPR report may be the model, the underlying transactional structure, upon which Coward works his comic manipulations.

There are other echoes of the SPR report scattered through the play: the stroke that killed her, Batten tells her interlocutors at one session, was prompted by an attack of rheumatic fever suffered after swimming (453); Elvira's death results from a case of pneumonia contracted after going out on the river and "getting soaked to the skin" (89). Batten says she often goes riding in the "other world" on a horse with "a very soft mouth" (361); Elvira will bitchily describe Ruth as having a "hard mouth," prompting Charles to complain that she shouldn't discuss Ruth "as though she were a horse" (70). Batten through Feda describes a frightening motor accident in 1914 in which she almost died (424–25); at the end of act 2, Ruth will in fact die in a motor accident, after Elvira, hoping to get Charles over with her in the spirit world, boobytraps the Condomine car and ends up with Ruth by mistake (81–82).

Yet a single passage on the last page of the report may represent the most direct link of all. Concerned to leave their readers convinced of the reality of the spirit world, Hall and Troubridge conclude by recollecting some remarkable sittings with Mrs. Leonard at which Feda revealed a knowledge of events "unknown to the sitters at the time" which later turned out to have taken place. They focus on several sessions from 1917 during which Feda transmitted a series of messages—not from Batten this time—but from a Mr. Benson, the dead father of a friend of Hall's named Daisy who was living in the Middle East. Initially, Feda's communications had puzzled them: while some of Mr. Benson's descriptions of his life on the "earth plane" fit in with what they knew of him, a number of them did not. Most strangely, Feda reported Benson as saying repeatedly,

From the mystic east: Hall in astrakahn collar, 1930s

"There were two of us that stood in the same relation to Daisy, but in a slightly different way" (539).

A subsequent exchange of letters with Daisy seemed to clarify the situation. Daisy, it was revealed, had had a stepfather (unknown to either Hall or Troubridge) who had in fact died just before the sittings at which Mr. Benson made himself known. Hall and Troubridge attributed the oddly mixed up messages transmitted by Feda at those sessions to the fact that "the Second Father himself was somewhere in the offing, crossing the line for a moment or two, flinging as it were his own mental pictures on to the screen, and that Feda thought they emanated from Mr. Benson, who lacked the skill to clear up the mistake" (541).

What is interesting about this episode—apart from the insight it gives once again into Hall and Troubridge's quite stunning faith in Mrs. Leonard's mediumistic powers—is the debate they report having afterward over one of its crucial details. Daisy, it turns out, had not known of her "Second Father's" death at the time of the sittings; in fact she only learned of it after Hall and Troubridge wrote to her. The purported Mr. Benson's curious statement from beyond, "There were two of us that stood in the same relation to Daisy"— which Hall and Troubridge both interpreted at the time as meaning "two of us here" (i.e., on the "Other Side")—likewise antedated any public announcement of the stepfather's death. How, Hall and Troubridge wondered, if the medium had been faking her transmissions, could she have known of the stepfather's death?

In an attempt to play devil's advocate, Hall reports, she tried suggesting to Troubridge that, grammatically speaking, the perplexing "Benson" statement did not necessarily imply that the stepfather was dead at the time of the sitting. Since Benson had known the "Second Father" in life and had in fact asked him to look after Daisy in the event of his own death, what could have been meant, Hall argued, was that he and the stepfather "stood in the same relation" to Daisy while both of them were still alive. But this interpretation prompts an immediate and imaginative rebuttal from Troubridge:

> I may say that Lady Troubridge had never any doubt that Mr. Benson's words must be taken as meaning that his old friend was dead at the date of the sitting. She argued in this way: "Supposing a man's *first wife* to be communicating with his *second* wife during a sitting, and the first wife when asked to define her relationship to the husband replied "there *were* two of us that *stood* in the same relation to Tom," and again "two of us *did* stand in the same relation to Tom," the sitter, being the second wife, might reasonably reply: "that is incorrect, because I did not stand in that relationship to Tom at the same time as you did, but I do stand in it now that you have ceased to do so." And this I think is quite logical. (345–46)

Logic aside—and the grammatico-metaphysical subtleties here are almost impossible to follow—the reader will grasp at once the argument's relevance to *Blithe Spirit*. In her hypothetical example, a "first wife" and "second wife" of the same man communicate (jealously) across the life-death divide: Troubridge might as well be describing the emotional dynamic in which she was involved with Hall and Batten. By giving the "second" wife the "logical" edge here —the second wife is polite yet forthright in defense of her overriding conjugal claim—Troubridge, who was often jealous of Hall's obsession with the dead Batten, may have been consciously or unconsciously asserting her own right, as Hall's living partner, to her deepest affection.[77] But her example is also a neat précis of the comic scenario of *Blithe Spirit*. Troubridge's remarks appear prominently in the next-to-last paragraphs of the report, with a number of important words italicized (*first wife*, *second*, and so on). One can imagine Coward alighting upon her "two-wife" minidrama and seeing its potential for marital comedy. Tom becomes Charles, the wives begin to embellish—farcically—on their distrust of each other, and the comic drama is born.

This is speculation, of course; one cannot prove that Coward read the SPR report, though evidence suggests he may well have. What seems less in doubt, however, is that one way or another he drew a significant part of his comic inspiration from Hall's notorious spiritual "three-way" with Troubridge and Batten. Yet this in itself may not be the whole story. For it can be argued that Hall's ghostly influence over the play may extend further. Up to this point I have said nothing about what *happens* in the comedy, once the basic scenario is established, nor have I alluded to the fact that after a series of seemingly Arcati-induced mishaps, including Ruth's accidental death and reappearance on the "Other Side"—from whence she and Elvira proceed to gang up on the hapless Charles—Charles ends up (apparently joyfully) with neither wife at the end. How to connect Coward's unromantic comic plot with the painfully romantic author of *The Well of Loneliness*?

The answer may lie in what *does* happen in *Blithe Spirit*. Like *The Well*, it can be read, I think, as a "gay plot," or homosexual parable, and not only because it evokes in a disguised fashion the curious love story of Hall and her two "wives." Emotionally, the story line is unorthodox—the opposite of a standard heterosexual "reconciliation" plot. In his 1981 book, *Pursuits of Happiness*, the noted film critic and philosopher Stanley Cavell describes what he calls the "comedy of remarriage" story line so often found in classic Hollywood films of the 1930s and 1940s: a divorced or estranged husband and wife, like a modern-day Titania and Oberon, squabble their way through a number of contentious scenes, only to be happily reunited in the end. The restoration of harmony is typically mediated by natural or supernatural influences: the alienated couple may return to a temporarily befuddling yet revivifying "green world" and be rejoined, as it were, by Nature itself, or one partner may resort to magical or pseudomagical forces in order to regain the other's affections. Prime examples of the remarriage plot for Cavell are the celebrated cinematic farces *Bringing Up Baby* (1938) and *The Philadelphia Story* (1940), starring Cary Grant and Katharine Hepburn, but the same plot pattern can be found in several Coward works, too—notably *Private Lives.*[78]

Though it opens in the orthodox comedy of remarriage fashion—with Charles and Ruth sparring—this is precisely the sort of plot *Blithe Spirit* does not become. The two bicker mercilessly. In act 1, Charles tells Ruth how "fascinating" the dead Elvira was; when Ruth refuses to be mollified by a "light, comradely kiss," he suggests half-seriously that they "get a divorce immediately" (16). But there will be no reconciliation. The supernatural is no help: with Elvira's abrupt reappearance their disaffection grows, even as Elvira plays them off against each other with wicked efficiency. And soon enough Elvira, too, is exasperated with Charles, who seems curiously unable to decide which wife he wants—the living one or the dead one—or indeed if he wants a wife at all. When Elvira and Ruth find themselves unexpectedly united on the "Other Side" after Ruth's death at the end of act 2, they immediately form a ghostly alliance against Charles, who responds with characteristically irritable comic sniping. By the end of the play this new homosocial arrangement—the two women together, the man alone—is in the ascendant. (Eager to have Ruth and Elvira leave his house, Charles grimly suggests that they go off and "take a cottage somewhere" [98]—like a pair of protoplasmic Ladies of Llangollen.) When

Madame Arcati, who has been trying for much of the play to get Elvira and Ruth to go back where they've come from, at last succeeds in making them invisible and unable to speak, they resort to crude poltergeistlike banging. Charles makes an extraordinary final speech, pledging to enjoy himself—without them—"as I've never enjoyed myself before":

> CHARLES [*softly*]: Ruth—Elvira—are you there? [*A pause*] Ruth—
> Elvira—I know damn well you're there—[*Another pause*] I just want
> to tell you that I'm going away so there's no point in your hanging
> about any longer—I'm going a long way away—somewhere where
> I don't believe you'll be able to follow. In spite of what Elvira said I
> don't think spirits can travel over water. Is that quite clear, my dar-
> lings? You said in one of your more acid moments, Ruth, that I had
> been hag-ridden all my life! How right you were—but now I'm
> free, Ruth dear, not only of Mother and Elvira, and Mrs. Winthrop-
> Lewellen, but free of you too, and I should like to take this farewell
> opportunity of saying I'm enjoying it immensely—[*A vase crashes
> into the fireplace*]. . . . Good-bye for the moment, my dears. I expect
> we are bound to meet again one day, but until we do I'm going to
> enjoy myself as I've never enjoyed myself before. You can break up
> the house as much as you like—I'm leaving it anyhow. Think
> kindly of me and send out good thoughts—[*The overmantel begins to
> shake and tremble as though someone were tugging at it*] Nice work,
> Elvira—perservere. Good-bye again—parting is such *sweet* sorrow!
> [*He goes out of the room just as the overmantel crashes to the floor and
> the curtain pole comes tumbling down.*]
>
> CURTAIN (108–9)

The parody of the "comedy of remarriage" here is complete—
even down to the mocking invocation of Shakespeare. Ruth and

Elvira are relegated to the oddly "sapphic" zone of the supernatural: Elvira's reappearance in the Condomine living room, we learn, was prompted not by Charles's subconscious desire but by certain bizarre psychic emanations from the housemaid, Edith. And Charles is propelled out of domesticity into a world without women, with all that that implies. As heterosexual bonds weaken and collapse, a new homosocial order is born.[79]

More openly than any other Coward comedy—including the supposedly "gay" but enigmatic *Design for Living* (1932)—*Blithe Spirit* can be read as an allegory of homosexualization. The allegory is overdetermined: Charles succeeds in divesting himself not just of one but of *two* heterosexual partners. Yet in this insistence on escape, the play may exhibit an autobiographical dimension. Just as Hall projected herself into Stephen Gordon in *The Well*, Coward seems to project himself into Charles Condomine. (Coward actually played the role of Condomine: despite having done no stage acting for six years, he took over the part from Cecil Parker during the London run in 1942.) Until now I've chosen to emphasize the link between Charles and doubly "married" Radclyffe Hall. Yet as Charles bids his giddy farewell to Ruth and Elvira, he functions less as a stand-in for Hall, one suspects, than for Coward himself. In his exhilarating rebuff to his two poltergeist wives, Charles seems to reject heterosexual decorum itself, just as the youthful Coward rejected the stultifying sexual conventions of lower-middle-class English life in the teens and 1920s.[80]

Less polemically than *The Well*, but just as decisively, then, *Blithe Spirit* reveals itself as a freedom fantasy. Norms are rejected— relegated to a spectral netherworld—and new configurations embraced. Coward, it is true, cannot be as brazenly "homosexual" about it as Hall was in her 1928 novel; the realities of censorship and his vulnerability as a closeted gay man make the liberating message

The ghosts of heterosexuality:
a) Coward as Charles Condomine (with Judy Campbell) in the 1942 production of *Blithe Spirit*
b) a binary curtain call, photographed by Cecil Beaton

in *Blithe Spirit* more veiled than a contemporary gay or lesbian reader might wish it to be. But in its drastic undoing of the marriage plot and final subversive open-endedness, the play bears more than a little resemblance to its fictional precursor. For all the misery that besets Stephen Gordon in *The Well*, there is an experimental "on-goingness" about her story, so that even at novel's end, bereft of Mary Llewellyn and their shared love, she seems set to launch herself into some unknown yet possibly more fulfilling world. Similarly, Charles Condomine, in the final scene of Coward's play, seems ready to move from a wrong world to a right one, toward his own proper destiny.

Was Coward at least partially inspired by Hall's literary example? That she has something to do with the gay plot of *Blithe Spirit* is suggested by the character about whom I've said least yet who is in a way the play's presiding "blithe" spirit—the irrepressible Madame Arcati. Madame Arcati might be said to occupy a symbolic position in *Blithe Spirit* similar to that of Brockett in *The Well*: she makes possible Charles's escape from the world of heterosexual routine. Absurd she may be, with her beads and crystals, outlandish seance outfits, and ludicrously inappropriate, games mistresslike exhortations ("What do you say we have another seance and really put our shoulders to the wheel?—Make it a real rouser!" [100]), but

One of the Arcatis:
playwright and novelist
Clemence Dane

within the fantastical world of the play, her mediumistic gifts are absolutely real. However obliviously, she is responsible—Puck-like—for everything that happens in the Condomine household. To the extent that she throws Charles's domestic arrangements into chaos, brings about the collapse of his marriage, and at the end lays the ghost(s) of heterosexual desire itself, she is instrumental to the play's allegory of homosexualization.

From one angle Madame Arcati is akin to the playwright himself; Coward's intricate magic results first in comic confusion, then in comic catharsis. Coward invests her with all of his own zany energy and comic ebullience. (He fantasized about playing her himself in the first London production.[81]) More than anything else, she keeps the tone of the play light, despite what might seem at first glance a morbid and misogynistic plot line. Yet he seems also to have had at least one real-life model for his brilliant creation. In his biography of Coward, his friend Cole Lesley suggests that Coward modeled Arcati in part on one of his closest female friends, the popular novelist and playwright Clemence Dane, whose real name was Winifred Ashton. Dane's "Junoesque" proportions, eccentric style of dress, and endearing conversational gaffes much entertained Coward during visits to her home in Tavistock Street, Covent Garden, in the late 1930s:

> [Coward] absolutely revelled, as we all did, in Winifred's Garden of Bloomers. The first I can remember was when poor Gladys [Calthrop] was made by Noël to explain to Winifred that she simply could not say in her latest novel, 'He stretched out and grasped the other's gnarled, stumpy tool.' The Bloomers poured innocently from her like an ever-rolling stream: 'Olwen's got crabs!' she cried as you arrived for dinner, or 'We're having roast cock tonight!' At the Old Vic, in the crowded foyer, she argued in ringing tones, 'But Joyce, it's well *known* that Shakespeare sucked Bacon dry.' . . . Schoolgirl slang

sometimes came into it, for she was in fact the original from whom Noël created Madame Arcati: 'Do you remember the night we all had Dick on toast?' she inquired in front of the Governor of Jamaica and Lady Foot. Then there was her ghost story: 'Night after night for weeks she tried to make him come . . . ' Why could she not have used the word 'materialise'? But then if she had we should never have had the fun.[82]

Dane, like Radclyffe Hall, seems to have been homosexual in emotional orientation: her first novel *Regiment of Women* (1917), about a young woman who becomes entangled with a seductive

Margaret Rutherford as
Madame Arcati in
Blithe Spirit, 1941

older female teacher, was apparently based on some of Dane's early experiences as student and teacher. Later in life, she lived for many years with a secretary-companion, Olwen Bowen, and Ben, "a neurotic and snappy fox-terrier who was as much disliked," says Cole Lesley, "as Olwen was loved." While Dane and Coward did not get to know one another well until the 1930s, they had always been part of the same homosexual artistic and theatrical circle. The stage producer Hugh "Binkie" Beaumont, Laurence Olivier, Katharine Cornell, her lover Nancy Hamilton, and the musical comedy star Mary Martin—not to mention Radclyffe Hall and Una Troubridge (who had hoped Dane would dramatize *The Well* in 1929)—were among the friends they shared.[83]

In basing Arcati partly on Dane, Coward might be said to pay tribute, once again, to that Lesbian Muse who—in her many different guises—was so much a part of his professional and imaginative life. Not surprisingly, by every hint that he can devise, he makes the jolly Arcati a raving English sapphist of the old school. (Certainly Margaret Rutherford plays her as such in the famous filmed version of the play from 1945.*) She is an unabashed spinster and, conversing with the Condomines in act 1, makes delicate yet insistent reference to a "great chum" (female) with whom she spends much of her time. When she is not crystal gazing, the tweedy-skirted medium likes bicycling up and down hills with butch abandon ("Steady rhythm—that's what counts. Once you get the knack of it you need never look back—on you get and away you go"); she is a

---

*Rutherford initially rejected the part of Madame Arcati because she took spiritualism and spirit mediums very seriously and thought Coward disrespectful. She always maintained that she played the part "straight"—that is, without any attempt at humor or satire. On Rutherford's own fascinating, often unconventional private life—she did not marry until she was fifty-two and then made what seems to have been *un mariage blanc*—see the memoir of her adoptive daughter, Dawn Langley Simmons, *Margaret Rutherford: A Blithe Spirit* (New York: McGraw-Hill, 1983). Rutherford adopted Simmons just before the latter—who grew up as a boy named Gordon—had permanent sex-change surgery.

devotee of field hockey and other rough girlish sports. Most amusingly, as she and Charles struggle together to dematerialize Elvira in act 3, she develops an infatuation for her invisible yet glamorous adversary. Smelling Elvira's "protoplasm" in the Condomine living room in act 3, she becomes violently excited ("Just a moment. I almost have contact—I can sense the vibrations—this is magnificent")—only to be overtaken with paroxysms when Elvira teasingly blows in her ear:

> MADAME ARCATI [*jumping*]: Yes, yes—again—again—
>
> ELVIRA [*blowing in the other ear behind MADAME ARCATI*]: How's that?
>
> MADAME ARCATI [*clasping and unclasping her hands in a frenzy of excitement*]: This is first rate—it really is first rate. Absolutely stunning! (87–88)

By the time Charles asks Arcati to leave the room so that he and Elvira can have a private chat, the besotted medium is "humming ecstatically" and blowing kisses toward the place in the room where she believes her "little darling" to be standing (88).

Yet like all great comic creations, Madame Arcati transcends any single living prototype. She is a motley, mercurial, strangely hermaphroditic presence in the play—an exquisite alchemical composite—and Radclyffe Hall is undoubtedly part of the characterological mix. Arcati of course represents an impossible combination of attributes: though calling herself a medium, she corresponds avidly with the Society for Psychical Research and keeps a notebook in which to jot down miscellaneous supernatural phenomena (62, 65). Members of the society prided themselves on being "scientific" researchers into the paranormal—neutral observers rather than paid practitioners of occult mysteries. (Charter members in 1882

Hall in beret

included the Cambridge physicists Sir William Crookes and Balfour Stewart, the classicist Gilbert Murray, Henry Sidgwick, and a number of other prominent intellectuals.[84]) Arcati's SPR connections sit oddly with her Blavatsky-like career as a medium. Indeed, were she to exist anywhere but the absurd world of farce, she would be a walking conflict of interest.

At those moments when Arcati seems to slip from the medium role to an investigator role—when she refers, for example, to the joint experiments she and her "great chum" have conducted in "telepathic hypnosis" (37), or brusquely interrupts Ruth Condomine's distressed account of Elvira's doings in act 2 to take down some notes ("Forgive this formality, but I shall have to make a report to the Psychical Research people")—we sense Coward gesturing, not so much at Clemence Dane or indeed Mrs. Leonard, but at the phantasmatic figure of Radclyffe Hall.* The Lesbian Muse, it turns out, is also, like Hall, a Psychical Researcher. And it is in the latter, positivistic guise—rather than her more mystic role—that Arcati saves the day. Drawing on the technical expertise she has gained as a ghost buster in "the Sudbury case" ("the case that made me famous"), she pinpoints the real cause behind Elvira's reappearance—the housemaid, Edith—and like a psychic troubleshooter, succeeds in dematerializing Elvira and Ruth with a minimum of fuss (102–106).

An attenuated tribute to Hall, perhaps—a matter of hints and jokes and the occasional mystic gleam—but a tribute, I think, nonetheless. For the inventive Madame Arcati indeed seems to

---

*Arcati's two comically contradictory styles of dress reinforce the sense one has of her split symbolic role: at the seance in act 1, in her medium guise, she wears "strange-looking gloves" and "barbaric" evening dress (21). Yet in ordinary life, as in act 2, when she comes to investigate the goings-on at the Condomines after the seance, she favors mannish tweed suits and a beret (60). Interestingly, there is a photo of Radclyffe Hall in precisely the latter sort of outfit, complete with beret, in a studio portrait from the late 1930s. During her last years, Hall's biographer Michael Baker writes, she took to wearing an "old French beret"; Troubridge wore it after Hall's death. See *Our Three Selves*, p. 348.

unleash something in Coward—some resistance to the comic status quo and the orthodoxies of sex and dramaturgy. It may be "reading too much in"—and too occult by half—but in the final scene between Charles and his rescuer, as a pooped but still exuberant Arcati is about to set off for home and Ovaltine, I cannot help but sense in Charles's thanks something of Coward's own gratitude—to Hall, for her taboo-shattering novel of 1928, and to the multitude of lesbian friends and colleagues who so enriched his life and art:

> MADAME ARCATI: Golly, what a night! I'm ready to drop in my tracks.
>
> CHARLES: Would you like to stay here?—there's the spare room, you know.
>
> MADAME ARCATI: No, thank you—each to his own nest—I'll pedal home in a jiffy—it's only seven miles.
>
> CHARLES: I'm deeply grateful to you, Madame Arcati. I don't know what arrangements you generally make but I trust you will send in your account in due course.
>
> MADAME ARCATI: Good heavens, Mr. Condomine—it was a pleasure—I wouldn't dream of such a thing.
>
> CHARLES: But I really feel that all those trances . . .
>
> MADAME ARCATI: I enjoy them, Mr. Condomine, thoroughly. I always have since a child.
>
> CHARLES: Perhaps you'd give me the pleasure of lunching with me one day soon?
>
> MADAME ARCATI: When you come back—I should be delighted.
>
> CHARLES: Come back?
>
> MADAME ARCATI [*lowering her voice*]: Take my advice, Mr. Condomine, and go away immediately.
>
> CHARLES: But, Madame Arcati! You don't mean that . . . ?

MADAME ARCATI: [*clearing her stuff from the table*]: This must be an unhappy house for you—there must be memories both grave and gay in every corner of it—also— [*She pauses*].

CHARLES: Also what?

MADAME ARCATI [*thinking better of it*]: There are more things in heaven and earth, Mr. Condomine. [*She places her finger to her lips.*] Just go—pack your traps and go as soon as possible.

CHARLES [*also in lowered tones*]: Do you mean that they may still be here?

MADAME ARCATI [*she nods and then nonchalantly whistles a little tune*]: Quien sabe, as the Spanish say. [*She collects her bag and her crystal.*]

CHARLES [*looking furtively around the room*]: I wonder—I wonder. I'll follow your advice, Madame Arcati. Thank you again.

MADAME ARCATI: Well, good-bye, Mr. Condomine—it's been fascinating—from first to last—fascinating. Do you mind if I take just one more sandwich to munch on my way home? [*Comes down to table for sandwich.*]

CHARLES: By all means. (107–108)

The homage here goes mostly unsaid—a sandwich is as good as a wink—but in this tolerant, amicable closure, Coward hints at a new kind of male-female alliance: between men who aren't husbands and women who aren't wives, but (blithe) kindred spirits to the last.

Radclyffe Hall died in October 1943; *Blithe Spirit* was still playing to full houses at London's Duchess Theatre at the time of her death.

(Una Troubridge would outlive her by almost twenty years, Coward by thirty.) It is unlikely Hall ever saw Coward's play: the last year of her life she was ill with severe eye and lung problems and spent much of her time in a nursing home in Bath. If she had seen it, would she have found the send-up of spiritualism offensive? One hopes not, for her sake. In its own antic way *Blithe Spirit* is both a testament—to those bonds of affection, camaraderie, and mutual respect that Hall and Coward somewhat improbably shared—and an authentic modern satire on the conventions of heterosexual romance. One hopes that she would have been capable of seeing the love—as well as the joke.

I began this essay by suggesting that to read Coward back "into" Hall's work, and Hall into Coward's, was to confuse the symbolic opposition between them—to make each one seem less himself or herself. Recognizing an allegorical subtext in *Blithe Spirit*— which is what recovering its ghostly allusions to Radclyffe Hall allows us to do—is a step on the way, of course, to a more "Hall-like" Noël Coward. Reading him with her in mind, he suddenly begins to look like a more resistant, rebarbative, even radical figure than he is usually taken to be: part of that great dissenting tradition of Anglo-American gay and lesbian literature initiated by Hall herself in *The Well of Loneliness.*[85]

At the same time that we contemplate a more Hall-like Coward, however, we may want to imagine a more Coward-like Hall. The familiar image of the novelist—grim and self-possessed, a martyr to the "invert" cause—depresses with its ideological, almost ecclesiastical, consistency. One wants her to have had a laugh now and then. Jonathan Brockett—witty, brazen, vernacular, the sort of character whom one can imagine inventing a Madame Arcati— gives one at least a partial hope that she did. Having Coward in the picture, if only fleetingly, seems to humanize her—to make her more

Noël Coward &
Radclyffe Hall

approachable. She may never be exactly sprightly: "Cowardizing" after the fact can only go so far, just as "Hallifying" Coward cannot diminish—let alone eradicate—his ultimately irresistible sense of fun. But she loses some of her heaviness and begins to move more freely across the literary landscape of the 1920s and 1930s.

Perhaps most important, however, the bonds between Hall and Coward (or Stephen and Brockett, or Madame Arcati and Charles Condomine) allegorize the rich yet neglected cultural relationships that have existed between gay men and lesbians in England and America since the turn of the century. The history of these relationships is instructive in itself—one's sense of an abysmal gap between gay and lesbian artistic traditions is at once undone—but full of a moral and political significance, too. Free from the mutual mishandlings and complaints seemingly endemic in heterosexual bonds, such cross-sex friendship may indeed be one of the most productive models we have for thinking about a nonpatriarchal world of social relations. They help us to practice for a less brutal future. Without question that apparently golden world of homosexual sociability through which Hall and Coward moved so elegantly and bravely in the 1920s and 1930s—with women as handsome as men and men as lovable as women—can prompt its own utopian, as well as nostalgic, visions.

And so on to a final (pictorial) allegory: a studio portrait of Radclyffe Hall—dressed as Noël Coward?—from 1932. In the single biography in which this photograph appears, it is captioned "a rare picture of John smiling." It is unique: Hall looks happy, self-forgetful, and more feminine, despite her clothing, than in any other surviving portrait. One suddenly remembers she was a woman after all. But the image also seems oddly incomplete, like a binary portrait

Uncanny resemblances: Hall and Coward in the early 1940s

Radclyffe Hall smiling, by Howard Coster, 1932

with one of its halves missing. Hall is turned to the side, her head tilted back; she is smiling—radiantly—at someone not in view. One suspects it isn't Una: the redoubtable Troubridge, though loyal to a fault, demanded that her consort-in-life-and-death be a husband and nothing else. Our eyes follow Hall's, ineluctably, into the empty air beyond the frame. And there we may find him—head tilted back in turn: the lover who wasn't, yet loved and was loved all the same.

Notes

1. Noël Coward's immense influence on Anglo-American cultural life in the twentieth century and exemplary role in the formation of what is now sometimes called gay sensibility have yet to be fully documented. Of the many books about him—including numerous memoirs by friends and acquaintances—the majority are by nonscholars and designed for popular consumption. The most helpful are Cole Lesley, *The Life of Noël Coward* (London: Jonathan Cape, 1976); Sheridan Morley, *A Talent to Amuse: A Biography of Noël Coward* (London: Pavilion Books, 1985); Clive Fisher, *Noël Coward* (London: Weidenfeld and Nicolson, 1992); Charles Castle, *Noël* (London: W. H. Allen, 1972); and Cole Lesley, Graham Payn, and Sheridan Morley, *Noël Coward and His Friends* (New York: William Morrow, 1979). Philip Hoare's *Noël Coward: A Biography* (London: Sinclair-Stevenson, 1995) appeared as my own book was going to press. Useful studies of the plays include John Lahr, *Coward the Playwright* (London: Methuen, 1982); Frances Gray, *Noël Coward* (London: Macmillan, 1987); Robert F. Kiernan, *Noël Coward* (New York: Ungar, 1986); Jacqui Russell, *File on Coward* (London and New York: Methuen, 1987); and Peter Holland, "Noël Coward and Comic Geometry," in Michael Cordner, Peter Holland, and John Kerrigan, eds., *English Comedy* (Cambridge, England: Cambridge University Press, 1994), 267–87. On Coward's songs and lyrics see Stephen Citron, *Noël and Cole: The Sophisticates* (London: Sinclair-Stevenson, 1992). For Coward's own impressions of his career see his numerous autobiographical writings—including the trilogy *Present Indicative* (1937), *Future Indefinite*

(1954), and the unfinished *Past Conditional* (published posthumously in 1986)—and Graham Payn and Sheridan Morley, eds., *The Noël Coward Diaries* (London: Weidenfeld and Nicolson, 1982).

Only recently have critics and biographers begun to explore in any detail the impact of Coward's sexuality—and his life as a mostly closeted gay man—on his art. Groundbreaking in this respect is Alan Sinfield's essay "Private Lives/Public Theater: Noël Coward and the Politics of Homosexual Representation," *Representations* 36 (Fall 1991): 43–63. Although occasionally inaccurate and somewhat hostile to Coward, Joseph Morella and George Mazzei's *Genius and Lust: The Creative and Sexual Lives of Cole Porter and Noël Coward* (New York: Carroll and Graf, 1995) helps explain how Coward's sexuality covertly informed both his stage persona and work as a playwright. Hoare's new biography is perhaps frankest of all on the vicissitudes of Coward's sex life.

2. See Susan M. Edwards, *Female Sexuality and the Law* (Oxford, England: Martin Robertson, 1981), pp. 43–45. For an account of the *Well* trial and its aftermath see Vera Brittain, *Radclyffe Hall: A Case of Obscenity?* (London: Femina Books, 1968), and Michael Baker, *Our Three Selves: The Life of Radclyffe Hall* (New York: William Morrow, 1985), pp. 223–49.

3. Radclyffe Hall, *The Well of Loneliness* (New York: Anchor, 1990), pp. 152–53. Subsequent notations in parentheses refer to page numbers in this edition.

4. Noël Coward, *The Lyrics of Noël Coward* (Woodstock, N.Y.: Overlook, 1983), pp. 105–106.

5. Coward's recording of "Any Little Fish Can Swim" can be found on the 1994 compilation, *The Master's Voice: Noël Coward—His HMV Recordings, 1928 to 1953* (Angel 0777 7 54919 2 0).

6. The purported dreariness of lesbians has a long history as a cultural topos, especially—paradoxically—among lesbians themselves. Camille Paglia, dubbed by one popular magazine "the 50-foot lesbian," has become famous for her antilesbian remarks ("When a man becomes gay, his I.Q. increases ten times; when a woman becomes lesbian, her I.Q. falls ten times"), but she is only the most recent sapphophobic sapphist. In a diary entry from 1930 cited in Hugo Vickers's *Loving Garbo: The Story of Greta Garbo, Cecil Beaton, and Mercedes de Acosta* (New York: Random House, 1994), Cecil Beaton described a conversation with Mercedes de Acosta, the renowned lesbian seductress and lover of both Garbo and Dietrich, in which de Acosta bemoaned "the dreary crowd of New York Lesbians and . . . made fun of their boring loyalty to one another, their earnestness, squalour, poverty & complete lack of humour" (p. 42). The bisexual novelist Elizabeth Bowen, whose discreetly lesbian novel *The Hotel* appeared a year before *The Well of Loneliness*, deplored what she called the "muffishness," "squashiness," and

"clagginess" of lesbian relationships. " 'Claggy,' " writes her biographer Victoria Glendinning, "was her expression for anything overanalytical, sentimental, sublimated, mawkish, maudlin. . . . Once, staying in Kerry with Norah Preece, she heard the young girls of the house announce that they were having such trouble with their boyfriends that they had decided to be 'toms.' Elizabeth and Eddy Sackville-West told them that on no account must they be toms: 'Always,' said Elizabeth, 'having terrible rows about bracelets.'" (*Elizabeth Bowen: A Biography* [New York: Alfred A. Knopf, 1977], p. 241).

And Daphne du Maurier—in love with Ellen Doubleday, the publisher's wife, and later with Noël Coward's stage partner Gertrude Lawrence—tried to convince the rather nervous Doubleday in 1948 that she (du Maurier) was not a lesbian: "Nobody could be more bored with all the 'L' people than I am." See Margaret Forster, *Daphne du Maurier* (London: Chatto & Windus, 1993), p. 229.

7. Mary Renault, "Afterword," *The Friendly Young Ladies* (New York: Pantheon, 1984), p. 281.

8. Ibid., p. 283.

9. Among other things, one of the novel's most obtuse characters—a conceited young doctor who tries unsuccessfully to seduce both of its lesbian heroines—is, like Hall, an ardent proponent of the theories of Freud and Havelock Ellis.

10. Cited in Lesley, *The Life of Noël Coward*, pp. 46–47.

11. See Noël Coward, *A Withered Nosegay: Three Cod Pieces* (1922; reprint, New York: Carroll and Graf, 1984), pp. 133, 181–87, and 225–39.

12. Lesley, Payn, and Morley, *Noël Coward and His Friends*, p. 199.

13. Coward was aware from an early age of the danger in Wildean self-disclosure. When he began his stage career as a child actor in 1911, memories of the Wilde case were still vivid: Coward's first patron, the actor-manager Charles Hawtrey, had in fact testified against Wilde at his 1895 trial. Coward's views on Wilde, at least as recorded by friends and biographers, reveal an interesting mixture of fellow feeling and contempt. "Oscar Wilde," writes Cole Lesley,

> irritated him beyond endurance, yet, as with Mary Queen of Scots, he bought and read every biography and memoir as they appeared and tormented himself all over again. As for the trial itself, the stupidity of everyone's behaviour—from Oscar Wilde, Lord Alfred Douglas and Lord Queensberry to the judge, jury, the press and the public—nearly drove him mad. The brilliant wit of the plays of course appealed to Noël, it was very much his own kind of wit; but the physical appearance and the character of Oscar Wilde repelled him. He was someone whom Noël would *not* have liked to meet, he said. The very idea of someone 'holding' the luncheon table with their wit until half past four was the antithesis of Noël's quick, short, spontaneous and unexpected comments, and he felt sure that Oscar Wilde's being consciously witty for hours on end would have bored him to death. (306)

Coward himself wrote the following in the 1940s:

> I read the unexpurgated *De Profundis*. Poor Oscar Wilde, what a silly, conceited, inadequate creature he was, and what a self-deceiver. It is odd that such brilliant wit should be allied to no humour at all. I didn't expect him to enjoy prison life and be speechless with laughter from morning to night, but he might have had a little warm human joke occasionally, if only with the Warder. The trouble with him was that he was a Beauty Lover, a podgy pseudophilosopher.

Cited in Lesley, *Life of Noël Coward*, p. 306.

Coward's determination to avoid a professional fate similar to Wilde's was entrenched. His two most important sexual relationships—with Jack Wilson in the 1920s and 1930s, and Graham Payn, who became his lover in 1945—were kept secret from the world; journalists were forbidden to mention his private life. True, he took the part of the bisexual Leo in the first New York production of *Design for Living* in 1933 and toward the end of his life—emboldened perhaps by the more liberal social attitudes of the the 1960s—played the part of the closeted homosexual novelist Hugh Latymer (whom he had modeled on Somerset Maugham) in the London and New York productions of his final play, *A Song at Twilight* (1966). Yet Clive Fisher and other biographers are no doubt correct to argue that Coward attempted to maintain a "facade of heterosexual correctness" in life and used his friendships with glamorous women such as Gertrude Lawrence and Marlene Dietrich to hide his homosexuality from the general public. See Fisher, *Noël Coward*, pp. 69–73, 222–23, and 246–54; Morella and Mazzei, *Genius and Lust*, pp. 246–55; and Hoare, *Noël Coward*, p. 417.

14. Lovat Dickson mentions Coward briefly in *Radclyffe Hall at the Well of Loneliness: A Sapphic Chronicle* (London: Collins, 1975), as does Baker in *Our Three Selves*. Among the Coward biographers, only Lesley, Payn, and Morley in *Noël Coward and His Friends* note the Hall connection: she is listed as being among the many famous visitors to Goldenhurst in the 1920s and 1930s.

15. Camille Paglia, "Homosexuality at the Fin de Siècle," *Sex, Art, and American Culture* (New York: Vintage, 1992), p. 24.

16. It would foolish to presume that homosexual men have been exempt from these misogynistic attitudes or, indeed, that sharing a sexual orientation inevitably results in cross-sex fellow feeling. Feminists have often argued, with some justice, that homosexual men can be as misogynistic as heterosexual men. (See, for example, Jane Marcus, *Virginia Woolf and the Languages of Patriarchy* [Bloomington: Indiana University Press, 1987], pp. 177, 181–86.) Certainly among Coward's contemporaries one can find any number of celebrated gay men who seem to have resisted any cross-sex homosexual solidarity. The composer Benjamin

Britten might be considered an antitype to Coward: as his biographer points out, not only was Britten estranged from his lesbian sister Barbara but he found lesbian or pseudolesbian display—as in the opening scene of Richard Strauss's opera *Der Rosenkavalier*—"loathsome" and claimed that it made him "physically sick." (See Humphrey Carpenter, *Benjamin Britten* [New York: Scribner's, 1992], pp. 44, 515–16.) Yet it remains my overall impression that such misogynistically grounded male homosexual "sapphophobia" is less common, less entrenched, and less destructive than sometimes presumed.

17. Here and elsewhere I am not particularly interested in "problematiz-ing"—as the lingo of contemporary theory would have it—the concepts of homosexuality, heterosexuality, or bisexuality. In speaking of someone as homosexual or lesbian—as I do when I write about Noël Coward or Radclyffe Hall—I mean to suggest simply that his or her erotic feelings were primarily directed toward members of the same sex. I remain skeptical about the possibility of any innately bisexual predisposition; most people, in my view, are predominantly heterosexual or homosexual. I am aware, however, that not everyone may share my prejudices or indeed my somewhat easy-going attitude toward nomenclature. For a discussion of philosophical and historical problems associated with contemporary terms relating to sexual object choice, see Judith Butler, "Imitation and Gender Insubordination," in Diana Fuss, ed., *Inside/Out: Lesbian Theories, Gay Theories* (New York and London: Routledge, 1991), pp. 13–31, and *Bodies That Matter: On the Discursive Limits of 'Sex'* (New York and London: Routledge, 1993); Martha Vicinus, " 'They Wonder to Which Sex I Belong': The Historical Roots of the Modern Lesbian Identity," *Feminist Studies* 18 (Fall 1992): 467–97; Jonathan Ned Katz, *The Invention of Heterosexuality* (New York: E. P. Dutton, 1995); and Marjorie Garber, *Vice Versa: Bisexuality and the Eroticism of Everyday Life* (New York: Simon and Schuster, 1995).

18. In the wake of Michael Holroyd's groundbreaking life of Lytton Strachey (1967), Quentin Bell's *Virginia Woolf* (1972), and Nigel Nicolson's *Portrait of a Marriage: V. Sackville-West and Harold Nicolson* (1973), three of the first biographical studies to open up the topic of cross-sex homosexual friendship, it has become increasingly clear how important such relationships have been in the intellectual and artistic life of the twentieth century. For further discussion of the couples mentioned, see, among others, Leon Edel, *Henry James* (Philadelphia: Lippincott, 1953–1972); Burdett Gardner, *The Lesbian Imagination, Victorian Style: A Psychological and Critical Study of 'Vernon Lee'* (New York: Garland, 1987); Denis Donoghue, *Walter Pater* (New York: Alfred A. Knopf, 1995); James R. Mellow, *Charmed Circle: Gertrude Stein and Company* (New York: Praeger, 1974); P. N. Furbank, *E. M. Forster: A Life* (New York and London: Harcourt Brace

Jovanovich, 1977); Brian Masters, *E. F. Benson* (London: Chatto & Windus, 1991); Gretchen H. Gerzina, *Carrington: A Life* (New York: W. W. Norton, 1989); Jane S. Smith, *Elsie de Wolfe: A Life in the High Style* (New York: Atheneum, 1982); Morella and Mazzei, *Genius and Lust*; Thadious M. Davis, *Nella Larsen: Novelist of the Harlem Renaissance* (Baton Rouge: Louisiana State University Press, 1994); Coleman Dowell, *A Star-Bright Lie* (Normal, Ill.: Dalkey Archive Press, 1993); Hugo Vickers, *Cecil Beaton: The Authorized Biography* (London: Weidenfeld and Nicolson, 1985) and *Loving Garbo*; Philip Herring, *Djuna: The Life and Work of Djuna Barnes* (New York: Viking, 1995); Millicent Dillon, *A Little Original Sin: The Life and Work of Jane Bowles* (New York: Holt, Rinehart and Winston, 1981); Claire Harman, *Sylvia Townsend Warner* (London: Chatto & Windus, 1989); Victoria Glendinning, *Edith Sitwell: A Unicorn Among Lions* (London: Weidenfeld and Nicolson, 1981); Janet Flanner, *Darlinghissima: Letters to a Friend*, ed. Natalia Danesi Murray (New York: Random House, 1985); George Wickes, *The Amazon of Letters: The Life and Loves of Natalie Barney* (New York: Putnam, 1976); Philippe Jullian and John Phillips, *Violet Trefusis: Life and Letters* (London: Hamilton, 1976); Violette Leduc, *La Bâtarde*, trans. Derek Coltman (New York: Farrar, Straus, and Giroux, 1965); Josyane Savigneau, *Marguerite Yourcenar: Inventing a Life*, trans. Joan E. Howard (Chicago and London: University of Chicago Press, 1993); and Gary Fountain and Peter Brazeau, *Remembering Elizabeth Bishop: An Oral Biography* (Amherst: University of Massachusetts Press, 1994). For a more personal and contemporary approach to the subject of friendship between gay men and lesbians, see Joan Nestle and John Preston, eds., *Sister and Brother: Lesbians and Gay Men Write About Their Lives Together* (San Francisco: HarperCollins, 1994).

19. Lesley, Payn, and Morley, *Noël Coward and His Friends*, p. 63.

20. Morley, *A Talent to Amuse*, p. 91.

21. Baker, *Our Three Selves*, p. 170.

22. Ibid., p. 225.

23. For more on Enthoven, see Coward, *Present Indicative* (Garden City, N.Y.: Doubleday, Doran, 1937), pp. 128, 131, 133, 139, and 144, and Baker, *Our Three Selves*, pp. 134 and 150. Enthoven later helped found the Theatre Museum in Covent Garden. On the Cave of Harmony—which opened in 1917 and counted among its habitués Katherine Mansfield, Evelyn Waugh, Vera Brittain, Aldous Huxley, Sylvia Townsend Warner, and the film director James Whale—see Douglas Goldring, *The 1920s: A General Survey and Some Personal Memories* (London: Nicholson and Watson, 1945), pp. 146–48, and Elsa Lanchester, *Elsa Lanchester Herself* (New York: St. Martin's, 1983), pp. 54–59.

24. Baker, *Our Three Selves*, p. 158.

25. Ibid., pp. 158–59. *On and Off*, an evocative oil sketch of Gerard on stage by the lesbian painter Gluck, is reproduced in Diana Souhami, *Gluck: Her Biography* (London: Pandora, 1988), p. 55.

26. The Goldenhurst guest book—with its hundreds of famous autographs—is now on permanent display at the Garrick Club in London. Lesbian friends and acquaintances who signed the book included Katharine Cornell, Nancy Hamilton, Elsa Maxwell, Dickie Fellows-Gordon, Winaretta Singer, and Nancy Spain. One can also find the signatures of Marlene Dietrich and Nesta Obermer, the lesbian painter Gluck's one-time lover.

27. Though several of his close friends volunteered to speak on behalf of *The Well* at its trial in 1928—including his Rye neighbor and fellow writer Sheila Kaye-Smith and the director Nigel Playfair—Coward maintained a discreet silence about the book in public.

28. Cited in Baker, *Our Three Selves*, pp. 267–68.

29. Sinfield, "Private Lives/Public Theater," p. 44.

30. See Kaier Curtin, *"We Can Always Call Them Bulgarians": The Emergence of Lesbians and Gay Men on the American Stage* (Boston: Alyson Publications, 1987), pp. 161–62.

31. On Porter's friendships with Elsie de Wolfe, Elisabeth Marbury, Elsa Maxwell, and many other well-known lesbian artists and performers, see Morella and Mazzei, *Genius and Lust*, pp. 30–31 and 90–94.

32. See du Maurier's lengthy paean to Lawrence ("She was a light that danced and swayed, that burned not with a dull lamp's steady glow but with all the divine uncertainty of flickering candles on a Christmas tree") in Sheridan Morley, *Gertrude Lawrence* (New York: McGraw-Hill, 1981), pp. xii and 172–73.

33. The term *male lesbian* is tendentious of course; yet surely we require more precise ways of talking about the kinds and degrees of male sapphophilia. Slang is no help. The rebarbative term *fag hag* exists—alas—to describe women who form intense attachments to gay men, but we have no comparable term for men, gay and straight, who gravitate instinctively toward lesbian women. The novelist Ernest Hemingway was one such man: his flamboyant heterosexualism and he-man pose masked a lifelong emotional obsession with homosexual women, including Gertrude Stein, whom he later savaged in *A Moveable Feast* (1964). (Once, after having an intense conversation with Stein about female homosexuality—or so he later bragged to Edmund Wilson—he became so sexually stimulated he went out and "fucked a lesbian with magnificent result.") He suspected his second wife, Pauline, of lesbian tendencies: their relationship may have partly inspired his strange short story "The Sea-Change" (1933), in which a woman leaves her male lover for another woman, and the unfinished, posthumously published novel *The Garden of Eden*

(1986), in which a husband and wife fall in love with the same young girl. For discussion of the links between Hemingway's sapphophilia and his art, see Marjorie Perloff, " 'Ninety Percent Rotarian': Gertrude Stein's Hemingway," *American Literature*, 62 (December 1990), 668–83; James R. Mellow, *Hemingway: A Life Without Consequences* (New York: Addison-Wesley, 1992), pp. 168, 231, 294, and 400; Mark Spilka, *Hemingway's Quarrel with Androgyny* (Lincoln: University of Nebraska Press, 1989); and Nancy R. Comley and Robert Scholes, *Hemingway's Genders: Rereading the Hemingway Text* (New Haven, Conn.: Yale University Press, 1994).

34. For an analysis of the "sexless" visual styles of the post-World War I period, see Sandra Gilbert and Susan Gubar, *No Man's Land: The Place of the Woman Writer in the Twentieth Century*, vol. 2, *Sexchanges* (New Haven, Conn.: Yale University Press, 1989), esp. ch. 8, "Cross-Dressing and Re-Dressing: Transvestism as Metaphor"; and Mary Louise Roberts, *Civilization Without Sexes: Reconstructing Gender in Postwar France, 1917–1927* (Chicago and London: University of Chicago Press, 1994).

35. Coward, *Present Indicative*, p. 338.

36. In a love letter to Obermer in 1937, Gluck wrote, "I think we are like a perfect apple cut in half—the most lovely and significant of fruits and I am sure for that reason chosen as of the Tree of Knowledge." See Souhami, *Gluck*, pp. 126 and 128. Coward and Obermer were acquainted; Obermer's signature appears in the Goldenhurst guest book for September 2, 1971.

37. The Seymour portrait is actually a composite based on separate photographs of Troubridge and Hall—a 1915 studio portrait of Troubridge, and the well-known image of Hall in cape and black sombrero now in the National Portrait Gallery in London.

38. Kiernan, *Noël Coward*, p. 14.

39. Mary Rennels, " 'Well of Loneliness' Now Republished Here," *New York Telegram Magazine*, December 15, 1928.

40. One cannot underestimate the influence of Hall's romantically conceived male impersonation on the development of twentieth-century high butch style. For a provocative reading of its multifarious psychological and cultural implications, see Esther Newton, "The Mythic Mannish Lesbian: Radclyffe Hall and the New Woman," *Signs: Journal of Women in Culture and Society*, 9 (Summer 1984), 557–75, reprinted in Martin Duberman, Martha Vicinus, and George Chauncey Jr., eds., *Hidden from History: Reclaiming the Gay and Lesbian Past* (New York: Meridian, 1989), pp. 281–93. Sandra Gilbert and Susan Gubar also comment insightfully on Hall's virile public style in *Sexchanges*, pp. 324–76, volume 2 of the trilogy *No Man's Land*, as does Katrina Rolley in "Cutting a Dash: The Dress of Radclyffe Hall and Una Troubridge," *Feminist Review* 35 (Summer 1990): 54–66.

On Mercedes de Acosta and Gluck, see Vickers, *Loving Garbo*, and Souhami, *Gluck*. De Acosta, writes Vickers, "always dressed in either black or white, or a combination of the two" and "favored cloaks, and tricorn hats, and well-cut jackets" (13). Greta Garbo later took to calling her "the little black and white" on account of her "austere" black clothes and white powdered face (116).

41. Hall, *Well of Loneliness*, p. 229. Though no single commentator has yet done full justice to its tremendous cultural influence and peculiar emotional power, a number of literary scholars, historians, and cultural critics have written illuminatingly on *The Well* during the past twenty-five years. Vera Brittain's retrospective account of the *Well* censorship trial, *Radclyffe Hall*, and Lovat Dickson's 1975 biography paved the way for a feminist reconsideration of Hall in the 1970s and 1980s; important early (and still useful) responses to the novel include Jane Rule's comments in *Lesbian Images* (New York: Doubleday, 1975), pp. 52–63; Catharine Stimpson, "Zero Degree Deviancy: The Lesbian Novel in English," *Critical Inquiry* 8 (1981): 363–80; and Claudia Stillman Franks, *Beyond 'The Well of Loneliness': The Fiction of Radclyffe Hall* (Amersham, Bucks: Avebury, 1982). Although brief, Michael Baker's comments on the novel in *Our Three Selves* (1985) are likewise sympathetic and well judged.

In the late 1970s, after Michel Foucault's call for a "history of sexuality," *The Well* began to attract attention from literary and cultural historians interested in late nineteenth- and early twentieth-century conceptions of homosexuality and the rise of modern notions of sexual identity. Important discussions of *The Well* from this perspective are to be found in Jeffrey Weeks, *Coming Out: Homosexual Politics in Britain from the Nineteenth Century to the Present* (London: Quartet, 1977), pp. 104–11, and *Sex, Politics, and Society: The Regulation of Sexuality Since 1800* (London: Longman, 1981), pp. 115–17; Lillian Faderman, *Surpassing the Love of Men: Romantic Friendship and Love Between Women from the Renaissance to the Present* (New York: William Morrow, 1981), pp. 317–23; Sonja Ruehl, "Inverts and Experts: Radclyffe Hall and the Lesbian Identity," in Rosalind Brunt and Caroline Rowan, eds., *Feminism, Culture and Politics* (London: Lawrence and Wishart, 1982), pp. 15–36; Esther Newton, "The Mythic Mannish Lesbian"; Jean Radford, "An Inverted Romance: *The Well of Loneliness* and Sexual Ideology," *The Progress of Romance* (London and New York: Routledge and Kegan Paul, 1986), pp. 97–111; and Jonathan Dollimore, "The Dominant and the Deviant: A Violent Dialectic," *Critical Quarterly* 28 (1986): 179–92, reprinted in Wayne R. Dynes and Stephen Donaldson, eds., *Homosexual Themes in Literary Studies* (New York and London: Garland, 1992), pp. 87–100.

Recently commentators have begun to approach the novel from a variety of new angles. In the sociologically oriented *Reflecting on 'The Well of Loneliness'*

(London and New York: Routledge, 1989), Rebecca O'Rourke discusses the popular reception of *The Well* and the ambivalent reaction the novel still evokes—especially among contemporary lesbians, for whom it remains necessary yet often infuriating reading. In "Below the Belt: (Un)Covering *The Well of Loneliness*," in Fuss, ed., *Inside/Out*, pp. 235–57, Michèle Aina Barale analyzes covers of successive editions of *The Well* for insights into changing popular interpretations of Hall's fiction over the past fifty years. And in *The Practice of Love: Lesbian Sexuality and Perverse Desire* (Bloomington and Indianapolis: Indiana University Press, 1994), Teresa de Lauretis, returning to Esther Newton's concept of the "mythic mannish lesbian" by way of Freudian and Lacanian theory, offers the most provocative psychoanalytic reading of Hall's novel to date.

Perhaps the least developed area of *Well* scholarship concerns the book's relation to its immediate literary context (the rich ferment of postwar Anglo-American women's writing) and its phenomenal impact on subsequent writers, male and female. But matters have begun to change, especially as more information about Hall and her literary contemporaries comes to light. In the delightfully titled " 'Unutterable Putrefaction and Foul Stuff': Two Obscene Novels of the 1920s," *Women's International Forum* 9 (1986): 341–56, Angela Ingram examines *The Well* in relation to several other "scandal" novels of the 1920s, including Michael Arlen's *The Green Hat* (1924) and Norah James's *Sleeveless Errand* (1929), a work parodied (along with *The Well*) in P. R. Stephensen's 1929 satire, *The Well of Sleevelessness*. In *Virginia Woolf* and "Sapphistry: The Woolf and the Well," in Karla Jay and Joanne Glasgow, eds., *Lesbian Texts and Contexts: Radical Revisions* (New York and London: New York University Press, 1990), pp. 164–81, Jane Marcus discusses Hall's ghostly influence on *A Room of One's Own* (1929) and other important Woolf texts. Illuminating comments on Hall and her artistic legacy can also be found in Shari Benstock's *Women of the Left Bank: Paris, 1900–1940* (Austin: University of Texas Press, 1986) and Gilbert and Gubar's three-volume *No Man's Land*. Finally, in my own literary-historical study, *The Apparitional Lesbian: Female Homosexuality and Modern Culture* (New York: Columbia University Press, 1993), I discuss *The Well* in relation to a number of nineteenth- and twentieth-century lesbian-themed works, including Charles Baudelaire's *Les fleurs du mal* (1857), Henry James's *The Bostonians* (1886), Compton Mackenzie's *Extraordinary Women* (1928), and Mary Renault's *The Friendly Young Ladies* (1944).

42. Baker, *Our Three Selves*, pp. 216–17.

43. See, for example, the "Personalities in Plasticine" head of Coward and the caricatures by Fernando Autori reproduced in Lesley, Payn, and Morley, *Noël Coward and His Friends*, pp. 92–93.

44. Cited in Russell, *File on Coward*, p. 28.

45. On the role of Marie Antoinette in nineteenth- and twentieth-century lesbian iconography, see Castle, *The Apparitional Lesbian*, pp. 107–49.

46. Lesley, *Life of Noël Coward*, p. 303.

47. Coward, *Present Indicative*, p. 107.

48. For an account of this curious work see Castle, *The Apparitional Lesbian*, pp. 136–40.

49. Coward, *A Withered Nosegay*, pp. 13–15. The work is a parody of sentimental turn-of-the-century tomes like Esther Singleton's *Famous Women Described by Great Writers* (New York: Dodd, Mead, 1904)—an anthology of potted biographies of celebrated or scandalous women, including Joan of Arc; Mary, Queen of Scots; Madame de Pompadour; Mrs. Fitzherbert; Isabella d'Este; and Caterina Cornaro, Queen of Cyprus.

50. Una, Lady Troubridge, *The Life of Radclyffe Hall* (New York: Citadel, 1963), p. 98.

51. Coward, *Lyrics of Noël Coward*, p. 238.

52. Ibid., pp. 232–33.

53. Emblematic of the new freedom wartime conditions brought lesbians is the case of Vita Sackville-West, who successfully masqueraded as a demobbed British soldier, "Julian," in London and Paris in 1918 and 1919 while carrying on a passionate love affair with Violet Trefusis. See Nicolson, *Portrait of a Marriage*, pp. 110–11, 152–53; and Glendinning, *Vita: The Life of V. Sackville-West* (New York: Alfred A. Knopf, 1983), pp. 95–97. For further discussion of the war's liberating psychological effect on homosexual women, see Sandra M. Gilbert, "Soldier's Heart: Literary Men, Literary Women, and the Great War," *Signs: Journal of Women in Culture and Society* 8 (1983): 422–50; Gilbert and Gubar, *No Man's Land*, vol. 2., pp. 291, 299–301, and 319; Susan Stanford Friedman, "Modernism of the 'Scattered Remnant': Race and Politics in H.D.'s Development," in Michael King, ed., *H.D.* (New York: National Poetry Foundation, 1986); and Benstock, *Women of the Left Bank*, pp. 24–28, 30–31.

54. On the proliferation of novels with lesbian themes in Britain during the 1920s, see Jeannette Foster, *Sex Variant Women in Literature*, 3d ed. (1956; reprint, Tallahassee, Fla.: Naiad, 1985), pp. 240–87.

55. Coward, *Semi-Monde* (1926), unpublished play script, I.ii.12. I am grateful to Michael Imison Playwrights Ltd. for making this script available to me.

56. See Wickes, *The Amazon of Letters*, pp. 63–64.

57. In his 1937 memoir *Present Indicative* Coward wrote the following of *Semi-Monde*:

> It was well-constructed and, on the whole, well-written; its production in London and New York seemed unlikely as some of the characters, owing to lightly suggested

abnormalities, would certainly be deleted by the censor; Max Reinhardt, however, was enthusiastic about it, and it was translated into German by Rudolph Kommer and taken in due course to Berlin, where for years it escaped production by a hair's breadth until eventually Vicky Baum wrote *Grand Hotel*, and *Semi-Monde*, being too closely similar in theme, faded gently into oblivion. (236)

Though not by any means one of his best plays, *Semi-Monde* was eventually produced, in 1977, after Coward's death, at the Citizens' Theatre, Glasgow, under the direction of Philip Prowse.

58. See Morley, *A Talent to Amuse*, p. 168.

59. Coward, *Spangled Unicorn*, in *A Withered Nosegay*, p. 251.

60. Ibid., pp. 251–52.

61. A sample of Hall's poetry, from the poem "Fruit of the Nispero," in *Poems of the Past and Present* (London: Chapman and Hall, 1910), p. 117:

> XVIII
>
> *Who may hold the soul of man or know it?*
> *Who may find the reason for its longings?*
> *Who may understand its sudden coming,*
> *Or the swiftness of its dim departure?*
> *I so much have loved my best beloved*
> *That her soul, responding to my kisses,*
> *Came and lay between my lips a moment,*
> *In the rapture of the happy darkness.*
> *Yet behold the morning saw it vanished,*
> *And I knew not what its form resembled.*
> *Even I, the happiest of lovers,*
> *May not solve the secret of its being.*

Noël Coward & Radclyffe Hall

62. Coward, *Spangled Unicorn*, p. 254. Hall and Troubridge shared Coward's dislike of Sitwell's poetic experiments: after she and Hall attended the first public performance of Sitwell and Walton's *Façade* in 1923, Troubridge wrote in her diary, "a *bad pain* afternoon of Miss Sitwell shouting down a megaphone." See Baker, *Our Three Selves*, p. 158.

63. Ibid., p. 259.

64. Coward, *The Lyrics of Noël Coward*, pp. 46–47.

65. Ibid., pp. 151–52.

66. For more information on Gladys Osborne Leonard, whom Arthur Conan Doyle described as "the greatest trance medium with whom [I] am acquainted," see Doyle, *The History of Spiritualism*, 2d ed. (New York: G. H. Doran, 1926), vol. 2, pp. 198–201; and Harry Price, *Fifty Years of Psychical Research: A Critical Survey* (London, New York, and Toronto: Longman's, Green, 1939), pp. 149–51 and 248. Leonard, who began life as a singer, claimed to have had visions

since childhood. She wrote two autobiographical works: *My Life in Two Worlds* (London: Cassell, 1931) and *The Last Crossing* (London: Cassell, 1937).

67. While under the "control" of Feda, Mrs. Leonard would take on the girl's voice and characteristics as if possessed. Writes Oliver Lodge, explaining Mrs. Leonard's technique, in *Raymond* (London: Methuen, 1916):

> Of mediumship there are many grades, one of the simplest forms being the capacity to receive an impression or automatic writing, under peaceful conditions, in an ordinary state; but the whole subject is too large to be treated here. Suffice it to say that the kind of medium chiefly dealt with in this book is one who, by waiting quietly, goes more or less into a trance, and is then subject to what is called 'control'—speaking or writing in a manner quite different from the medium's own normal or customary manner, under the guidance of a separate intelligence technically known as 'a control,' which some think must be a secondary personality which indeed certainly *is* a secondary personality of the medium, whatever that phrase may really signify—the transition being effected in most cases quite easily and naturally. In this secondary state, a degree of clairvoyance or lucidity is attained quite beyond the medium's normal consciousness, and facts are referred to which must be outside his or her normal knowledge. The control, or secondary personality which speaks during the trance, appears to be more closely in touch with what is popularly spoken of as 'the next world' than with customary human existence, and accordingly is able to get messages through from people deceased; transmitting them through the speech or writing of the medium, usually with some obscurity and misunderstanding, and with the mannerisms belonging either to the medium or the control. (86–87)

68. Radclyffe Hall and Una, Lady Troubridge, "On a Series of Sittings with Mrs. Osborne Leonard," *Proceedings of the Society for Psychical Research*, 78 (December 1919): 339–554. Subsequent page references are noted parenthetically. The report on the Leonard sittings was not Hall and Troubridge's only contribution to the psychical research literature; two years later they published "A Veridical Apparition," *Journal of the Society for Psychical Research*, 20 (April 1921): 78–88, an account of Hall's sighting of the apparition of a friend in a garage in Brighton in 1920. Despite the backing of Lodge and others, however, Hall and Troubridge's relations with the Society for Psychical Research (SPR) were troubled, and several of the society's leading lights viewed the two women with suspicion on account of their lesbianism. In anticipation of the *Well* scandal, a male member of the society's governing council, St. George Lane Fox-Pitt, objected to Hall's joining the council in 1920 on the ground that she was an "immoral woman." Hall won the resulting slander action brought against him but not without a fair amount of unpleasant publicity. See Baker, *Our Three Selves*, pp. 122–31.

69. Hall and Troubridge were by no means the only homosexually inclined women involved with the occult in the years before and after the First World War.

From its beginnings the spiritualist movement attracted sexually unconventional women. The renowned theosophist Madame Blavatsky (1831–1891) is rumored to have been homosexual: she despised the thought of sex with men ("To Hades with this sex love! It is a beastly appetite that should be starved into submission") and later in life lived with a devoted female companion and disciple, the Countess Constance Wachtmeister. The well-known Oxford couple Charlotte Moberly and Eleanor Jourdain, principal and vice principal of St. Hugh's at the turn of the century, were believers in ghosts, telepathy, and time travel: in 1911 they published a sensational book together in which they described seeing an apparition of Marie Antoinette at Versailles in 1901. And other turn-of-the-century women, such as Havelock Ellis's lesbian wife Edith Lees Ellis, and Edith Somerville, of the popular Irish writing duo Somerville and Ross, used spiritualism to affirm their devotion to dead female partners. With the help of a medium, Ellis communed for many years with her lover Lily after Lily's death in 1903; Somerville maintained her relationship with Violet Martin ("Martin Ross") after Martin's death in 1915. Somerville even continued publishing novels under both of their names: she claimed to receive daily inspirational communications from "Ross" through a planchette. See John Symonds, *The Lady with the Magic Eyes: Madame Blavatsky—Medium and Magician* (New York: Thomas Yoseloff, 1960), pp. 220–24; Sylvia Cranston, *HPB: The Extraordinary Life and Influence of Helena Blavatsky, Founder of the Modern Theosophical Movement* (New York: Putnam's, 1993), pp. 45, 291–95; Castle, *The Apparitional Lesbian*, pp. 107–49; Maurice Collis, *Somerville and Ross* (London: Faber and Faber, 1968), pp. 176–84; and Phyllis Grosskurth, *Havelock Ellis* (New York: Alfred A. Knopf, 1980), pp. 211–12. On the psychological appeal spiritualism held for women in general in the later nineteenth and early twentieth century—and especially its link to early feminism and the women's suffrage movement—see Alex Owen, *The Darkened Room: Women, Power, and Spiritualism in Late Nineteenth-Century England* (London: Virago, 1989) and Ann Braude, *Radical Spirits: Spiritualists and Women's Rights in Nineteenth-Century America* (Boston: Beacon, 1989).

70. See Lesley, *Life of Noël Coward*, p. 18.

71. See *Weatherwise*, in Coward, *Collected Sketches and Lyrics* (London: Hutchinson, 1931); and *Still Life*, scene 2, and *Present Laughter*, act 2, scene 1, in Coward, *Play Parade*, vol. 4 (London: Heinemann, 1954). Note too the following well-known verses from "The Stately Homes of England" (1937):

> The Stately Homes of England,
> Though rather in the lurch,
> Provide a lot of chances
> For Psychical Research—
> There's the ghost of a crazy younger son

Who murdered, in thirteen fifty-one,
An extremely rowdy Nun
Who resented it,
And people who come to call
Meet her in the hall.
The baby in the guest wing,
Who crouches by the grate
Was walled up in the west wing
In fourteen twenty-eight.
If anyone spots
The Queen of Scots
In a hand-embroidered shroud
We're proud
Of the Stately Homes of England.

See *Lyrics of Noël Coward*, pp. 189–90.

72. Noël Coward, *Three Plays: Blithe Spirit, Hay Fever, Private Lives*. (New York: Grove, 1965). All further references to *Blithe Spirit* are to this edition, with page numbers noted parenthetically.

73. See Baker, *Our Three Selves*, p. 262.

74. See *Blithe Spirit*, pp. 344–45. In describing Feda's whimsical personality at length, Hall and Troubridge followed Lodge's lead in *Raymond*. Lodge first mentions Feda in a transcription of notes from a sitting in 1915: "Mrs. Leonard went into a sort of trance, I suppose, and came back as a little Indian girl called 'Freda,' or 'Feda,' rubbing her hands and talking in the silly way they do." Elsewhere he describes her typical way of manifesting herself: "Feda soon arrived, said good evening, jerked about on the chair, and squeaked or chuckled, after her manner when indicating pleasure." See *Raymond*, pp. 120 and 192.

75. Baker, *Our Three Selves*, p. 98.

76. Typically Feda acted as a spiritual go-between, describing things said and done by Batten, who was unable to "control" Mrs. Leonard directly. But one can find interesting variations on this behavior. Occasionally Batten seems somehow to manipulate Feda in a way that causes Mrs. Leonard to move in response. An example is described on p. 421 of the SPR report: the invisible Batten "pushes" Feda, in order to demonstrate the "pitching" motion that occurred when she, Batten, was involved in a car accident in 1915, and Mrs. Leonard "jerks up and forward almost out of her seat." On very rare occasions, Feda is displaced entirely, and Batten briefly inhabits Mrs. Leonard's body herself:

> The first personal control attempted by A.V.B. took place on January 19th, 1917. I [Hall] was taking the sitting alone, and my attention was first called to the fact that something unusual was about to occur by Feda, who fidgeted uncomfortably,

exclaiming at the same time: "What *are* you trying to do, Ladye, what *are* you trying to do?" After these words, no more was heard of Feda, the medium remaining perfectly still, and apparently, deeply entranced, for what I should say was the space of a minute or two. When she began to speak again she did so in an almost inaudible whisper, her first words being: "Where are you? Pull me forward." There was nothing evidential in this first A.V.B. control, as speech appeared very difficult and movement almost impossible. A certain amount of emotion was shown, but, on the whole, admirable self-control was maintained on the part of the purporting communicator, which was again very characteristic of A.V.B. who was extremely self-controlled during her life-time. Since January 19th, 1917, there have been repeated efforts at an A.V.B. control, which has been very slowly growing in power and evidential value. (479)

This may seem (marginally) clear, but elsewhere the metaphysical situation is more difficult to grasp. In the following "A.V.B. control" Batten seems simultaneously inside and outside Mrs. Leonard's body:

> During the early A.V.B. controls, A.V.B. complained that she could not make the medium laugh. One day, however, she suddenly succeeded in doing so, and what ensued was extraordinarily reminiscent of A.V.B.'s own laugh, and this characteristic laugh has, since then, often occurred. On several occasions the timbre of Mrs. Leonard's voice has changed, and has become very like A.V.B.'s voice; startlingly so, once or twice. A.V.B. herself has remarked upon this, which appears only to be possible during the earlier part of the personal controls. On one occasion A.V.B. said disconsolately: "Oh! now the power is going, can't you hear my voice getting Mrs. Leonardy again?" which statement was correct. *(480)*

At such moments one cannot help viewing Mrs. Leonard's accomplishments cynically—as a clever charade in response to Hall and Troubridge's undoubtedly revealing unconscious gestures.

77. On Troubridge's jealousy of Batten, whom Hall idolized, see Baker, *Our Three Selves*, pp. 96–97 and 102–103.

78. Stanley Cavell, *Pursuits of Happiness: The Hollywood Comedy of Remarriage* (Cambridge, Mass.: Harvard University Press, 1981). For a further exploration of Coward's plot patterns—and their relation to classic Shakespearean and Jonsonian precedents—see Holland, "Noël Coward and Comic Geometry."

79. Amy Farmer makes a similar point in her comments on the play in Claude J. Summers, ed., *The Gay and Lesbian Literary Heritage* (New York: Henry Holt, 1995), p. 177. The 1945 film version of *Blithe Spirit*, directed by David Lean, to some degree "reheterosexualizes" the denouement by having Charles killed off in an accident in the final frames and plumped down between the two women (who remain visible in ghostly guise) as a new spirit. The Hollywoodish suggestion here is that the henpecked Charles will now be stuck between the dueling wives forever

and that this is somehow what he really desires. In the play, however, Coward, who accused Lean of having "fucked up the best thing I ever wrote," is forthright about Charles's antiromantic feelings and makes a point of showing—in the following scene with Madame Arcati, in which the two of them are struggling to send Ruth and Elvira back to the "Other Side"—that Charles has had nothing to do with either of their spectral reappearances:

MADAME ARCATI: Now then, Mr. Condomine—the discussion—fire away.

CHARLES: Well, my wives and I have been talking it over and they are both absolutely convinced that I somehow or other called them back.

MADAME ARCATI: Very natural.

CHARLES: I am equally convinced that I did not.

MADAME ARCATI: Love is a strong psychic force, Mr. Condomine—it can work untold miracles. A true love call can encompass the universe—

CHARLES [*hastily*]: I'm sure it can, but I must confess to you frankly that, although my affection for both Elvira and Ruth is of the warmest, I cannot truthfully feel that it would come under the heading that you describe.

ELVIRA: I should just think not indeed.

MADAME ARCATI: You may not know your own strength, Mr. Condomine.

CHARLES [*firmly*]: I did *not* call them back—either consciously or subconsciously.

MADAME ARCATI: But, Mr. Condomine . . .

CHARLES: That is my final word on the subject. (101)

The subsequent discovery of the gormless Edith's unconscious agency—the housemaid turns out to be "a Natural—just the same as the Sudbury case" (105)—confirms both Charles's intuition that he is not to blame and the classically "sapphic" nature of supernatural agency. Here Coward follows one of the axioms of nineteenth- and early twentieth-century psychical research lore: that psychically receptive females (and adolescent girls in particular) were the usual "cause" of spectral apparitions or telekinetic activity in a household. See Owen, *The Darkened Room*, and Braude, *Radical Spirits*.

80. Coward's sexual sophistication, allied to his love of theater, manifested itself early on. Reminiscing about the time they both appeared as child actors in a production of *Peter Pan* directed by Dion Boucicault, the Irish actor Micheal MacLiammóir observed that

Noël really wasn't like a child at all—he lacked the quality. I don't mean he was an unnatural, preposterously precocious, forward or unpleasant child at all. But to other children he seemed totally grown-up. He was decidedly puckish, witty, dry, clipped and immensely competent. I remember once during *Peter Pan* Noël and I were asked to tea by a horrible old man who lived in Earls Court and I said I didn't want to go much; Noël said nor did he, but he thought we ought to because it was good for business to be invited out. I looked at him with a kind of religious terror: at fourteen he knew it all. (Cited in Morley, *A Talent to Amuse*, p. 25)

Philip Hoare suggests that Coward's adolescent relationship with Philip Streatfeild, an artist fifteen years his senior, may have been a sexual one. See *Noël Coward*, pp. 32–37.

81. See Fisher, *Noël Coward*, p. 150.

82. Lesley, *Life of Noël Coward*, pp. 227–28.

83. See Coward, *Future Indefinite*, pp. 90–91, and Lesley, *Life of Noël Coward*, pp. 227, 372–73. For more on Dane, whom the West End theater producer Binkie Beaumont once described as "the Lady Blessington and Madame de Sévigné of Covent Garden," see Richard Huggett, *Binkie Beaumont: Éminence Grise of the West End Theatre, 1933–1973* (London: Hodder and Stoughton, 1989), pp. 138–45 and 252–56, and Joanne Shattuck, ed., *The Oxford Guide to British Women Writers* (Oxford, England, and New York: Oxford University Press, 1993), pp. 126–27.

84. See Ruth Brandon, *The Spiritualists: The Passion for the Occult in the Nineteenth and Twentieth Centuries* (Buffalo, N.Y.: Prometheus, 1984), pp. 87–88, and Dickson, *Radclyffe Hall*, pp. 80–81.

85. For all the humor in *Blithe Spirit*, some contemporaries found Coward's pointed critique of marriage a bit unsettling. After the London opening, one reviewer, Ivor Brown, complained in the July 9, 1941, issue of *Punch* that "Mr. Coward's touch deserts him when he makes Mr. Condomine gloat over his new-found freedom from women." Only the madcap caperings of Margaret Rutherford as Madame Arcati, by establishing the play as a piece of "riotous nonsense," kept it from turning into a "fatally sour kind of fun." Some of the uneasiness can undoubtedly be attributed to the fact that the play takes death and the dead—quite literally—as its comic subject. Aware of its anomalous emotional register, Coward himself referred to *Blithe Spirit*, oxymoronically, as a "light comedy about death." But some of the discomfort aroused, it seems to me, can also be attributed to its radical rejection of heterosexual convention.

References

Arlen, Michael. *The Green Hat*. 1924. Rpt., London: Cassell, 1968.

Baker, Michael. *Our Three Selves: The Life of Radclyffe Hall*. New York: William Morrow, 1985.

Barale, Michèle Aina. "Below the Belt: (Un)Covering *The Well of Loneliness*." In Diana Fuss, ed., *Inside/Out: Lesbian Theories, Gay Theories*, pp. 235–57. New York and London: Routledge, 1991.

Barnes, Djuna. *Ladies Almanack*. 1928. Rpt., Elmwood Park, Ill.: Dalkey Archive Press, 1992.

——. *Nightwood*. 1936. Rpt., New York: New Directions, 1946.

Bell, Quentin. *Virginia Woolf: A Biography*. New York: Harcourt Brace Jovanovich, 1972.

Benson, E. F. *Make Way for Lucia*. New York: Thomas Y. Crowell, 1977.

Benstock, Shari. *Women of the Left Bank: Paris, 1900–1940*. Austin: University of Texas Press, 1986.

Bowen, Elizabeth. *The Hotel*. London: Constable, 1927.

Brandon, Ruth. *The Spiritualists: The Passion for the Occult in the Nineteenth and Twentieth Centuries*. Buffalo, N.Y.: Prometheus, 1984.

Braude, Ann. *Radical Spirits: Spiritualism and Women's Rights in Nineteenth-Century America*. Boston: Beacon, 1989.

Brittain, Vera. *Radclyffe Hall: A Case of Obscenity?* London: Femina Books, 1968.

Butler, Judith. "Imitation and Gender Insubordination." In Diana Fuss, ed., *Inside/Out: Lesbian Theories, Gay Theories*, pp. 13–31. New York and London: Routledge, 1991.

——. *Bodies That Matter: On the Discursive Limits of "Sex"*. New York and London: Routledge, 1993.

Carpenter, Humphrey. *Benjamin Britten*. New York: Scribner's, 1992.

Castle, Charles. *Noël*. London: W. H. Allen, 1972.

Castle, Terry. *The Apparitional Lesbian: Female Homosexuality and Modern Culture*. New York: Columbia University Press, 1993.

Cavell, Stanley. *Pursuits of Happiness: The Hollywood Comedy of Remarriage*. Cambridge, Mass.: Harvard University Press, 1981.

Citron, Stephen. *Noël and Cole: The Sophisticates*. London: Sinclair-Stevenson, 1992.

Collis, Maurice. *Somerville and Ross*. London: Faber and Faber, 1968.

Comley, Nancy R. and Robert Scholes. *Hemingway's Genders: Rereading the Hemingway Text*. New Haven, Conn.: Yale University Press, 1994.

Coward, Noël. *Chelsea Buns*. London: Hutchinson, 1925.

——. *Semi-Monde*. Unpublished play script, 1926.

——. *Collected Sketches and Lyrics*. London: Hutchinson, 1931.

——. *Play Parade*. 6 vols. London: Heinemann, 1934–1962.

——. *Present Indicative*. Garden City, N.Y.: Doubleday, Doran, 1937.

——. *Future Indefinite*. London: W. Heinemann, 1954.

——. *Three Plays: Blithe Spirit, Hay Fever, Private Lives*. New York: Grove Press, 1965.

——. *The Noël Coward Diaries*. Ed. Graham Payn and Sheridan Morley. London: Weidenfeld and Nicolson, 1982.

——. *The Lyrics of Noël Coward*. Woodstock, N.Y.: Overlook, 1983.

——. *A Withered Nosegay: Three Cod Pieces*. 1922. Rpt., New York: Carroll and Graf, 1984.

——. *Past Conditional*. London: Methuen, 1986.

——. *The Collected Stories of Noël Coward*. New York: E. P. Dutton, 1987.

——. *The Master's Voice: Noël Coward—His HMV Recordings 1928 to 1953*. Angel 0777 7 54919 2 0. 1994.

Cranston, Sylvia. *HPB: The Extraordinary Life and Influence of Helena Blavatsky, Founder of the Modern Theosophical Movement*. New York: Putnam, 1993.

Curtin, Kaier. *"We Can Always Call Them Bulgarians": The Emergence of Lesbians and Gay Men on the American Stage*. Boston: Alyson, 1987.

Dane, Clemence [Winifred Ashton]. *Regiment of Women*. 1917. Rpt., London: Heinemann, 1966.

Davis, Thadious M. *Nella Larsen: Novelist of the Harlem Renaissance.* Baton Rouge: Louisiana State University Press, 1994.

De Lauretis, Teresa. *The Practice of Love: Lesbian Sexuality and Perverse Desire.* Bloomington and Indianapolis: Indiana University Press, 1994.

Dickson, Lovat. *Radclyffe Hall at the Well of Loneliness: A Sapphic Chronicle.* London: Collins, 1975.

Dillon, Millicent. *A Little Original Sin: The Life and Work of Jane Bowles.* New York: Holt, Rinehart and Winston, 1981.

Dollimore, Jonathan. "The Dominant and the Deviant: A Violent Dialectic." *Critical Quarterly* (1986) 28: 179–92. Reprinted in Wayne R. Dynes and Stephen Donaldson, eds., *Homosexual Themes in Literary Studies,* pp. 87–100. New York and London: Garland, 1992.

Donoghue, Denis. *Walter Pater.* New York: Alfred A. Knopf, 1995.

Dowell, Coleman. *A Star-Bright Lie.* Normal, Ill.: Dalkey Archive Press, 1993.

Doyle, Arthur Conan. *The History of Spiritualism,* 2d ed. New York: G. H. Doran, 1926, vol. 2.

Duberman, Martin, Martha Vicinus, and George Chauncey Jr., eds., *Hidden from History: Reclaiming the Gay and Lesbian Past.* New York: Meridian, 1989.

Edel, Leon. *Henry James.* 5 vols. Philadelphia, Pa.: J. W. Lippincott, 1953–72.

Edwards, Susan M. *Female Sexuality and the Law.* Oxford: Martin Robertson, 1981.

Faderman, Lillian. *Surpassing the Love of Men: Romantic Friendship and Love Between Women from the Renaissance to the Present.* New York: William Morrow, 1981.

Farmer, Amy. "Noël Coward." In Claude J. Summers, ed., *The Gay and Lesbian Literary Heritage.* New York: Henry Holt, 1995.

Finlayson, Iain. *The Sixth Continent: A Literary History of Romney Marsh.* New York: Atheneum, 1986.

Firbank, Ronald. *The Flower Beneath the Foot.* 1923. Rpt., Harmondsworth, Middlesex, England: Penguin, 1986.

Fisher, Clive. *Noël Coward.* London: Weidenfeld and Nicolson, 1992.

Flanner, Janet. *Darlinghissima: Letters to a Friend.* Ed. Natalia Danesi Murray. New York: Random House, 1985.

Forster, Margaret. *Daphne du Maurier.* London: Chatto & Windus, 1993.

Foster, Jeannette. *Sex Variant Women in Literature.* 1956. Rpt., 3d ed. Tallahassee, Fla.: Naiad, 1985.

Fountain, Gary and Peter Brazeau. *Remembering Elizabeth Bishop: An Oral Biography.* Amherst: University of Massachusetts Press, 1994.

Franks, Claudia Stillman. *Beyond 'The Well of Loneliness': The Fiction of Radclyffe Hall*. Amersham, Bucks: Avebury, 1982.

Friedman, Susan Stanford. "Modernism of the 'Scattered Remnant': Race and Politics in H.D.'s Development." In Michael King, ed., *H.D.* New York: National Poetry Foundation, 1986.

Furbank, P. N. *E.M. Forster: A Life*. New York and London: Harcourt Brace Jovanovich, 1977.

Garber, Marjorie. *Vice Versa: Bisexuality and the Eroticism of Everyday Life*. New York: Simon and Schuster, 1995.

Gardner, Burdett. *The Lesbian Imagination, Victorian Style: A Psychological and Critical Study of "Vernon Lee"*. New York: Garland, 1987.

Gerzina, Gretchen H. *Carrington: A Life*. New York: W. W. Norton, 1989.

Gilbert, Sandra M. "Soldier's Heart: Literary Men, Literary Women, and the Great War." *Signs: Journal of Women in Culture and Society* 8 (1983): 422–50.

Gilbert, Sandra and Susan Gubar. *No Man's Land: The Place of the Woman Writer in the Twentieth Century*, vol. 2, *Sexchanges*. New Haven, Conn.: Yale University Press, 1989.

Glendinning, Victoria. *Elizabeth Bowen: A Biography*. New York: Alfred A. Knopf, 1977.

——. *Edith Sitwell: A Unicorn Among Lions*. London: Weidenfeld and Nicolson, 1981.

——. *Vita: The Life of V. Sackville-West*. New York: Alfred A. Knopf, 1983.

Goldring, Douglas. *The 1920s: A General Survey and Some Personal Memories*. London: Nicholson and Watson, 1945.

Gray, Frances. *Noël Coward*. London: Macmillan, 1987.

Grosskurth, Phyllis. *Havelock Ellis*. New York: Alfred A. Knopf, 1980.

Hall, Radclyffe. *'Twixt Earth and Stars*. London: John and Edward Bumpus, 1906.

——. *A Sheaf of Verses*. London: John and Edward Bumpus, 1908.

——. *Poems of the Past and Present*. London: Chapman and Hall, 1910.

——. *Songs of Three Counties and Other Poems*. London: Chapman and Hall, 1913.

——. *The Forgotten Island*. London: Chapman and Hall, 1915.

——. *The Forge*. London: J. W. Arrowsmith, 1924.

——. *The Unlit Lamp*. 1924. Rpt., London: Virago, 1981.

——. *Adam's Breed*. London: Cassell, 1926.

——. *Miss Ogilvy Finds Herself*. London: W. Heinemann, 1934.

——. *A Saturday Life*. 1925. Rpt., London: Virago, 1987.

——. *The Well of Loneliness*. 1928. Rpt., New York: Anchor, 1990.

Hall, Radclyffe and Una, Lady Troubridge. "On a Series of Sittings with Mrs. Osborne Leonard." *Proceedings of the Society for Psychical Research* 78 (December 1919): 339–554.

———. "A Veridical Apparition." *Journal of the Society for Psychical Research* 20 (April 1921): 78–88.

Harman, Claire. *Sylvia Townsend Warner: A Biography*. London: Chatto & Windus, 1989.

Herring, Philip. *Djuna: The Life and Work of Djuna Barnes*. New York: Viking, 1995.

Hoare, Philip. *Noël Coward: A Biography*. London: Sinclair-Stevenson, 1995.

Holland, Peter. "Noël Coward and Comic Geometry." In Michael Cordner, Peter Holland, and John Kerrigan, eds., *English Comedy*, pp. 267–87. Cambridge: Cambridge University Press, 1994.

Holroyd, Michael. *Lytton Strachey: A Critical Biography*. 2 vols. London: W. Heinemann, 1967–68.

Huggett, Richard. *Binkie Beaumont: Éminence Grise of the West End Theatre 1933–1973*. London: Hodder and Stoughton, 1989.

Huneker, James. *Painted Veils*. New York: Liveright, 1920.

Hyde, Catherine [pseud.], ed. *Secret Memoirs of Princess Lamballe*. Washington, D.C. and London: M. Walter Dunne, 1901.

Ingram, Angela. " 'Unutterable Putrefaction and Foul Stuff': Two Obscene Novels of the 1920s." *Women's International Forum* 9 (1986): 341–56.

James, Norah. *Sleeveless Errand*. New York: William Morrow, 1929.

Jullian, Philip and John Phillips. *Violet Trefusis: Life and Letters*. London: Hamilton, 1976.

Katz, Jonathan Ned. *The Invention of Heterosexuality*. New York: Dutton, 1995.

Keane, Molly. *Devoted Ladies*. 1934. Rpt., London: Virago, 1984.

Kiernan, Robert F. *Noël Coward*. New York: Ungar, 1986.

Lahr, John. *Coward the Playwright*. London: Methuen, 1982.

Lanchester, Elsa. *Elsa Lanchester Herself*. New York: St. Martin's, 1983.

Leduc, Violette. *La Bâtarde*. Trans. Derek Coltman. New York: Farrar, Straus, and Giroux, 1965.

Lehmann, Rosamond. *Dusty Answer*. New York: Henry Holt, 1927.

Leonard, Gladys Osborne. *My Life in Two Worlds*. London: Cassell, 1931.

———. *The Last Crossing*. London: Cassell, 1937.

Lesley, Cole. *The Life of Noël Coward*. London: Jonathan Cape, 1976.

Lesley, Cole, Graham Payn, and Sheridan Morley. *Noël Coward and His Friends*. New York: William Morrow, 1979.

Lewis, Wyndham. *The Apes of God*. London: Arthur Press, 1930.

Lodge, Oliver. *Raymond: or Life and Death, with Examples of the Evidence for Survival of Memory and Affection After Death.* 2d ed. London: Methuen, 1916.

Mackenzie, Compton. *Extraordinary Women: Theme and Variations.* London: Martin Secker, 1928.

Mander, Raymond and Joe Mitchenson. *Theatrical Companion to Coward.* London: Rockcliff, 1957.

Marcus, Jane. *Virginia Woolf and the Languages of Patriarchy.* Bloomington: Indiana University Press, 1987.

——. "Sapphistry: The Woolf and the Well." In Karla Jay and Joanne Glasgow, eds., *Lesbian Texts and Contexts: Radical Revisions,* pp. 164–81. New York and London: New York University Press, 1990.

Masters, Brian. *E. F. Benson.* London: Chatto & Windus, 1991.

Mellow, James R. *Charmed Circle: Gertrude Stein and Company.* New York: Praeger, 1974.

——. *Hemingway: A Life Without Consequences.* New York: Addison-Wesley, 1992.

Melville, Joy. *Ellen and Edy: A Biography of Ellen Terry and Her Daughter, Edith Craig, 1847–1947.* London and New York: Pandora, 1987.

Morella, Joseph and George Mazzei. *Genius and Lust: The Creative and Sexual Lives of Cole Porter and Noël Coward.* New York: Carroll and Graf, 1995.

Morley, Sheridan. *Gertrude Lawrence.* New York: McGraw-Hill, 1981.

——. *A Talent to Amuse: A Biography of Noël Coward.* London: Pavilion Books, 1985.

Nestle, Joan and John Preston, eds. *Sister and Brother: Lesbians and Gay Men Write about Their Lives Together.* San Francisco: HarperCollins, 1994.

Newton, Esther. "The Mythic Mannish Lesbian: Radclyffe Hall and the New Woman." *Signs: Journal of Women in Culture and Society* 9 (Summer 1984): 557–75. Reprinted in Martin Duberman, Martha Vicinus and George Chauncey Jr., eds., *Hidden from History: Reclaiming the Gay and Lesbian Past,* pp. 281–93. New York: Meridian, 1989.

Nicolson, Nigel. *Portrait of a Marriage: V. Sackville-West and Harold Nicolson.* New York: Atheneum, 1973.

O'Rourke, Rebecca. *Reflecting on 'The Well of Loneliness'.* London and New York: Routledge, 1989.

Owen, Alex. *The Darkened Room: Women, Power and Spiritualism in Late Nineteenth-Century England.* London: Virago, 1989.

Paglia, Camille. "Homosexuality at the Fin de Siècle." *Sex, Art, and American Culture,* pp. 22–25. New York: Vintage, 1992.

Payn, Graham and Sheridan Morley, eds. *The Noël Coward Diaries.* London: Weidenfeld and Nicolson, 1982.

Perloff, Marjorie. " 'Ninety Percent Rotarian': Gertrude Stein's Hemingway." *American Literature* 62 (December 1990): 668–83.

Price, Harry. *Fifty Years of Psychical Research: A Critical Survey*. London, New York, and Toronto: Longman's, Green, 1939.

Radford, Jean. "An Inverted Romance: *The Well of Loneliness* and Sexual Ideology." *The Progress of Romance*, pp. 97–111. London and New York: Routledge and Kegan Paul, 1986.

Renault, Mary. "Afterword." *The Friendly Young Ladies*. New York: Pantheon, 1984.

Rennels, Mary. " 'Well of Loneliness' Now Republished Here." *New York Telegram Magazine*, December 15, 1928.

Roberts, Mary Louise. *Civilization Without Sexes: Reconstructing Gender in Postwar France, 1917–1927*. Chicago and London: University of Chicago Press, 1994.

Rolley, Katrina. "Cutting a Dash: The Dress of Radclyffe Hall and Una Troubridge." *Feminist Review* 35 (Summer 1990): 54–66.

Royde-Smith, Naomi. *The Tortoise-Shell Cat*. London: Constable, 1925.

Ruehl, Sonja. "Inverts and Experts: Radclyffe Hall and the Lesbian Identity." In Rosalind Brunt and Caroline Rowan, eds., *Feminism, Culture, and Politics*, pp. 15–36. London: Lawrence and Wishart, 1982.

Rule, Jane. *Lesbian Images*. New York: Doubleday, 1975.

Russell, Elizabeth. *The Enchanted April*. 1922. Rpt., London: Virago, 1986.

Russell, Jacqui. *File on Coward*. London and New York: Methuen, 1987.

Sackville-West, Vita. *Seducers in Ecuador*. London: Hogarth, 1924.

Savigneau, Josyane. *Marguerite Yourcenar: Inventing a Life*. Trans. Joan E. Howard. Chicago and London: University of Chicago Press, 1993.

Shairp, Mordaunt. *The Green Bay Tree*. Boston: Baker International Play Bureau, 1933.

Shattuck, Joanne, ed. *The Oxford Guide to British Women Writers*. Oxford, England, and New York: Oxford University Press, 1993.

Simmons, Dawn Langley. *Margaret Rutherford: A Blithe Spirit*. New York: McGraw-Hill, 1983.

Sinfield, Alan. "Private Lives/Public Theater: Noël Coward and the Politics of Homosexual Representation." *Representations* 36 (Fall 1991): 43–63.

Singleton, Esther. *Famous Women Described by Great Writers*. New York: Dodd, Mead, 1904.

Smith, Jane S. *Elsie de Wolfe: A Life in the High Style*. New York: Atheneum, 1982.

Souhami, Diana. *Gluck: Her Biography*. London: Pandora, 1988.

Spilka, Mark. *Hemingway's Quarrel with Androgyny*. Lincoln: University of Nebraska Press, 1989.

Stephensen, P. R. *The Well of Sleevelessness.* London: Scholartis Press, 1929.

Stimpson, Catharine. "Zero Degree Deviancy: The Lesbian Novel in English." *Critical Inquiry* 8 (1981): 363–80.

Summers, Claude J., ed. *The Gay and Lesbian Literary Heritage.* New York: Henry Holt, 1995.

Symonds, John. *The Lady with the Magic Eyes: Madame Blavatsky—Medium and Magician.* New York: Thomas Yoseloff, 1960.

Troubridge, Una, Lady. *The Life of Radclyffe Hall.* New York: Citadel, 1963.

Vicinus, Martha. " 'They Wonder to Which Sex I Belong': The Historical Roots of the Modern Lesbian Identity." *Feminist Studies* 18 (Fall 1992): 467–97.

Vickers, Hugo. *Cecil Beaton: The Authorized Biography.* London: Weidenfeld and Nicolson, 1985.

——. *Loving Garbo: The Story of Greta Garbo, Cecil Beaton, and Mercedes de Acosta.* New York: Random House, 1994.

Warner, Sylvia Townsend. *Lolly Willowes.* 1926. Rpt., Chicago: Academy Chicago, 1978.

——. *Summer Will Show.* 1936. Rpt., London: Virago, 1987.

Weeks, Jeffrey. *Coming Out: Homosexual Politics in Britain from the Nineteenth Century to the Present.* London: Quartet, 1977.

——. *Sex, Politics, and Society: The Regulation of Sexuality Since 1800.* London: Longman, 1981.

Wickes, George. *The Amazon of Letters: The Life and Loves of Natalie Barney.* New York: Putnam, 1976.

Woolf, Virginia. *Mrs. Dalloway.* New York: Harcourt Brace, 1925.

——. *Orlando.* London: Hogarth, 1928.

——. *Between the Acts.* London: Hogarth, 1941.

Yeats-Brown, Francis. *The Lives of a Bengal Lancer.* New York: Viking, 1930.

Author's collection, 28; British Film Institute, 100; British Library, 4, 5; Cutter Collection and Mary Evans Picture Library, 75 (bottom); Estate Brassaï, 50; Fine Arts Society, 29 (top), 36 (top); Garrick Club and E. T. Archive, 22; Glasgow Museums: Art Gallery and Museum, Kelvingrove, 63; Harry Ransom Humanities Research Center and the Estate of Radclyffe Hall, 34 (top and bottom left), 35 (top), 82, 89, 103, 108 (bottom); Hulton Deutsch Collection, 15 (bottom), 17, 27, 32 (top), 86; Illustrated London News Picture Collection, 74 (top); Mary Evans Picture Library, 75 (top); Michael Parkin Gallery, 61; National Portrait Gallery, 35 (bottom), 59, 110; Papers of Mercedes de Acosta, Rosenbach Museum and Library, Philadelphia, Pennsylvania, 36 (bottom); Raymond Mander and Joe Mitchenson Theatre Collection, 15 (top), 19 (right), 32 (bottom), 41, 84, 98, 108 (top); Society for Psychical Research and Mary Evans Picture Library, 79; Sotheby's London, Cecil Beaton Archive, 45, 96, 97; Stanford Libraries, 5, 16, 18, 21, 26, 29, 34 (bottom right), 37, 40, 44, 54, 64, 69, 74 (bottom), 80; Victoria and Albert Museum, 19 (left)

Index

Between Men ~ Between Women
Lesbian and Gay Studies
Lillian Faderman and Larry Gross, Editors

Edward Alwood, *Straight News: Gays, Lesbians, and the News Media*

Corinne E. Blackmer and Patricia Juliana Smith, editors, *En Travesti: Women, Gender Subversion, Opera*

Alan Bray, *Homosexuality in Renaissance England*

Joseph Bristow, *Effeminate England: Homoerotic Writing After 1885*

Claudia Card, *Lesbian Choices*

Joseph Carrier, *De Los Otros: Intimacy and Homosexuality Among Mexican Men*

John Clum, *Acting Gay: Male Homosexuality in Modern Drama*

Gary David Comstock, *Violence Against Lesbians and Gay Men*

Laura Doan, editor, *The Lesbian Postmodern*

Allen Ellenzweig, *The Homoerotic Photograph: Male Images from Durieu/ Delacroix to Mapplethorpe*

Lillian Faderman, *Odd Girls and Twilight Lovers: A History of Lesbian Life in Twentieth-Century America*

Linda D. Garnets and Douglas C. Kimmel, editors, *Psychological Perspectives on Lesbian and Gay Male Experiences*

Richard D. Mohr, *Gays/Justice: A Study of Ethics, Society, and Law*

Sally Munt, editor, *New Lesbian Criticism: Literary and Cultural Readings*

Timothy F. Murphy and Suzanne Poirier, editors, *Writing AIDS: Gay Literature, Language, and Analysis*

Noreen O'Connor and Joanna Ryan, *Wild Desires and Mistaken Identities: Lesbianism and Psychoanalysis*

Don Paulson with Roger Simpson, *An Evening in the Garden of Allah: A Gay Cabaret in Seattle*

Judith Roof, *Come As You Are: Sexuality and Narrative*

Judith Roof, *A Lure of Knowledge: Lesbian Sexuality and Theory*

Claudia Schoppmann, *Days of Masquerade: Life Stories of Lesbians During the Third Reich*

Alan Sinfield, *The Wilde Century: Effeminacy, Oscar Wilde, and the Queer Moment*

Chris Straayer: *Deviant Eyes, Deviant Bodies: Sexual Re-Orientations in Film and Video*

Kath Weston, *Families We Choose: Lesbians, Gays, Kinship*

Kath Weston, *Render me, Gender Me: Lesbians Talk Sex, Class, Color, Nation, Studmuffins . . .*

Carter Wilson, *Hidden in the Blood: A Personal Investigation of AIDS in the Yucatán*

Designer: Euangkham Chuaviriya
Text: Granjon
Compositor: Columbia University Press
Printer: Edwards Brothers
Binder: Edwards Brothers